Table of Contents

Practice Test #1

Practice Questions

Literature and Language Studies

1. The graphic below is probably being used to teach which concept?

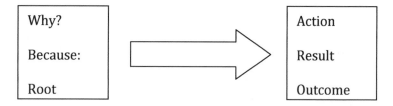

   a. Character analysis
   b. Cause and effect
   c. Compare and contrast
   d. Symbolism

2. Why is phonemic awareness critical to early literacy development?
   a. It is critical to understanding the alphabetic principle
   b. Students who cannot understand the context of stories will not be able to comprehend them
   c. Understanding and identifying the component sounds of words is an essential prerequisite skill for understanding phonics
   d. Students who cannot write letters are unlikely to be able to recognize them

3. A words correct per minute (WCPM) test would most likely be used by a reading teacher to...
   a. Determine whether a student meets state reading standards
   b. Conduct a preliminary screening of a student's reading fluency
   c. Test a student's reading comprehension skills
   d. Assess a student's mastery of a unit on functional texts

4. Which of the following distinguishes literary texts from informational texts?
   a. The author's intent (to entertain or inform)
   b. The richness of the vocabulary used (informal or formal)
   c. The reading level (easy or difficult)
   d. The length (long or short)

5. Poems are generally divided into...
   a. Haikus
   b. Iambic pentameters
   c. Sonnets
   d. Stanzas

6. A newspaper article about globalization is accompanied by an image of a young child in ragged, dirty clothing begging in front of a shiny, modern office building. This image is most likely intended to illustrate which of the following ideas?

a. Rapid construction occurs in some cities as a result of globalization

b. The education system in the country where the photo was taken is inadequate to sustain its current rate of economic development

c. Globalization has exacerbated economic inequality in many parts of the world

d. Globalization has reduced the infant mortality rate

7. Which of the following activities is most helpful in developing general literacy skills of English language-learners or other students who are not yet reading fluently?

a. Solely focus on phonetics and building knowledge of sight words; without these skills, students will never be truly literate.

b. Assign partners or "buddies," allowing the language-learners to observe and learn from more literate classmates.

c. Allow students to participate verbally in class activities without grading or giving undue critique to reading or written work.

d. Set goals with each student during each assignment to allow them to feel a sense of accomplishment and gradually increase the level of challenge throughout the year.

8. If a student is reading a text aloud at an "instructional level," he or she should:

a. Find no more than one in five questions difficult to read.

b. Find no more than one in ten questions difficult to read.

c. Comprehend the majority, if not all, of what he reads.

d. Be able to instruct or teach other students to read and understand the text.

9. Which choice is the best way for a teacher to help students build their bank of sight words and vocabulary?

a. Using flash cards to drill and retain a large quantity of words.

b. Assign a wide variety of reading texts to introduce and familiarize students with words in different contexts.

c. Encourage parents to read with their children to help them learn new words and build motivation to read.

d. Provide each child with a dictionary and thesaurus to use during class work and homework and encourage them to explore word usage.

10. Mr. Blankenship, a 7th-grade language arts teacher, is planning class work related to comprehension of non-fiction writing. Which of the following skills should he introduce in order to help students build comprehension?

a. Text annotation

b. Rewriting text in your own words

c. Previewing and summarizing information

d. Making an outline

11. Which of the following statements are most true regarding emergent readers?

a. Emergent readers are very well-suited for demonstrating fluent, expressive oral reading to their peers and are very confident serving as peer tutors. They show that they are ready for this role by appearing to 'emerge' from literacy instruction with confidence and excitement.

b. Emergent readers benefit from instruction across all aspects of literacy acquisition, including word identification, phonics, writing, listening, and speaking; they are still in the process of acquiring language skills in all forms and may be working at varied skill levels.

c. Emergent readers learn best when given the opportunity to listen and observe other students reading and speaking. Teachers should make efforts to ask the students to observe and listen as much as possible before attempting to read and write independently.

d. Emergent readers often display very high aptitudes in other disciplines, especially Social Studies and the Sciences. They have the innate ability to connect information from one class to the next.

12. Which student listed below exhibits signs of needing special instruction due to a learning disability or delay?

a. Jenna, a 6th-grade student who pauses to sound out long words with multiple syllables, slowing her oral reading.

b. Alina, whose thick accent makes her speech very difficult to understand when reading aloud or giving presentations.

c. Gavin, a 5th-grader who often does not remember concepts he has previously learned.

d. Billy, an 8th-grade student who frequently fails to turn in writing assignments and will sometimes skip over test questions that involve writing.

13. Which of the following choices is not a component of reading fluency?

a. Speed

b. Comprehension

c. Accuracy

d. Voice Modulation

14. Which of the following assessments would be best for matching students to appropriately challenging books?

a. Ask the student to read aloud the vocabulary words listed on the back of the book to make sure that they can read most of them.

b. Choose reading books with suggested grade levels on the front cover.

c. Allow students to choose books that are "not too easy and not too hard."

d. Use the same grade-level book to help all students practice and achieve the same skills.

15. Which of the following statements accurately characterizes expectations for written and spoken language in the classroom?

a. It is reasonable to hold students to the same formal grammatical standards whether they are speaking or writing

b. It is reasonable to expect the same level of grammatical accuracy whether the student is writing a first draft or a final product

c. Students should be expected to use a richer vocabulary when speaking than when writing

d. Students' final drafts should be held to higher grammatical standards than their informal speech or their early drafts

16. Which of the following statements is true of word analysis?
    a. Word analysis is the same as decoding, and can be taught through direct instruction in phonics
    b. Word analysis can be taught by explicitly modeling the thought processes used to infer the meaning of a word
    c. Word analysis is a higher-order skill that is not necessary for school-age students
    d. Word analysis cannot be successful unless students can memorize all of the many prefixes, roots, and suffixes used in the English language

17. Which of the following activities demonstrates an effective use of oral language practice to facilitate reading comprehension?
    a. Students take turns reading aloud from a text ("round-robin" reading)
    b. Students read aloud together from a text (choral reading)
    c. Students practice pronouncing unfamiliar vocabulary words from a text, and then read the text aloud
    d. Students discuss what they already know about the subject of a text they're about to read in order to activate prior knowledge

18. When instructing an ESL student who is already literate in his native language, reading teachers should...
    a. Assume that the student already understands the alphabetic principle because it characterizes all written languages
    b. Expect that the student already has experience with reading a phonetically irregular language because all languages have extensive phonetic irregularities
    c. Consider that there is significant diversity among the basic operating principles of written languages, and that there may be central principles of written English with which the student is unfamiliar
    d. Assume that the student has no frame of reference for the alphabetic principle or the phonetic irregularities of written English

19. Mrs. Cornelius has arranged a conference with her daughter's teacher, Mr. Wilson. At the conference, Mrs. Cornelius says she has noticed that even though her daughter, Chloe, can decode individual words with little trouble, she moves her lips when she reads silently and displays no expression when she reads aloud. She also shows very little comprehension of what she has read. Based on these observations, Mr. Wilson should suggest that Chloe's main problem is...
    a. Decoding
    b. Reading fluency
    c. Reading comprehension
    d. Blending

20. In selecting texts for silent reading in the classroom, teachers should...
    a. Select a range of texts, including some above and below grade level, to accommodate students with varying ability levels
    b. Select only texts at their students' grade level, but include different types of texts covering a wide range of topics
    c. Focus on constructing multiple series of texts on particular subjects
    d. Select texts that are either at or slightly below grade level, and that feature topics of interest for the students so that they will enjoy silent reading more

21. A 4th grade class will begin a unit next week in which students will be building oral language concepts through a variety of readings, projects and discussions. Which of the following genres would be most appropriate to use for reading text and class discussion?
    a. Fiction
    b. Folk tale
    c. Biography
    d. Science fiction

22. There are some students in Mr. Everly's class that do not speak aloud in class discussions on a regular basis. Class discussions tend to be dominated by a smaller group of more outspoken students. How should he address this circumstance?
    a. No action is necessary.
    b. Make a rule that each student must contribute at least once to class discussion before a student can speak a second time.
    c. Verbally encourage the quieter students to speak during class time, telling them that their contributions are valuable.
    d. Use group work to engage students in conversation, observing and encouraging quieter students in this context.

23. Which of the following instructional techniques would be most appropriate for building and monitoring students' listening skills?
    a. Read a story, poem, or other piece of literature to them each day before beginning class.
    b. Give pop quizzes on the day's lessons at the end of class.
    c. Preview concepts that will be introduced in class and then allow the students to answer recall-based questions verbally at the end of class.
    d. Pay close attention to the students' answers on tests when they relate to classroom discussions.

24. Which choice is most true regarding the relationship of listening skills to literacy development?
    a. One of the last stages of literacy development is the honing of listening skills.
    b. Once a student learns to read, it is unnecessary to practice listening comprehension.
    c. Before students can become literate in any sense, they must be able to listen carefully to reading instruction.
    d. Listening skills and comprehension are integral to literacy and should continue to be developed simultaneously with other literacy skills.

25. Mrs. Baines' 6th-grade class is preparing for their "World Community" project in which each student selects a famous person from another country to research and report upon. The student will compile research into a written report and create a poster with interesting pictures and visual images related to that person. The students will also deliver a speech or series of quotations originally spoken by their research subject. Why would Mrs. Baines include this last portion of the project?
    a. To help her students get ready for the play they will put on later in the year, practicing speaking another person's words with expression and interest.
    b. To help students connect individual identity and oral expression while thinking about the world from another person's perspective.
    c. To provide material for the listening recall and comprehension portions of the unit quizzes and tests.
    d. To round out a project that is predominantly focused on reading and writing by adding a bit of speech into the requirements.

26. Aaron is chosen to read aloud in class today. His teacher finds it interesting that he struggles with words that have many graphemes, but few syllables. Which set of words did he misread?
   a. Symphony, measure, chicken
   b. Few, belt, halt
   c. Auditorium, cacophony, friendliness
   d. Hesitant, knowing, built

27. Which of the following choices shows the best way to utilize technology in the writing process?
   a. The student uses a personal voice recorder to record ideas in stream-of-consciousness. The student can then use the recording to transcribe thoughts into writing.
   b. The student uses a word processor to begin writing from start to finish.
   c. The student videotapes class discussions and views them in order to organize information regarding the topic.
   d. The student uses an online graphic organizer to arrange the topic, main ideas, and supporting evidence into an outline, from which he can begin to write.

28. A 6th-grade class is beginning its first-ever independent research project, in which the teacher assigns points of intervention to scaffold student efforts. At what point should the teacher first meet with the student to help him or her with the inquiry process?
   a. Choosing a topic
   b. Gathering and selecting appropriate sources
   c. Forming an outline
   d. Writing a rough draft

29. Which of the following describes the best way to incorporate research and individual inquiry into weekly class work?
   a. Students visit the library or media center once a week to explore and check out books.
   b. Students are asked to bring an article or essay from a newspaper, magazine, or academic website each week to share with the class.
   c. Students complete a small section of a research project each week in class.
   d. Whenever a question is posed during class discussion, a student can volunteer to research the answer in the library or online in the classroom.

30. Amanda is a 6th grade student who has been diagnosed with a receptive language disorder. As a direct result of her disability, which of the following tasks is she is most likely to have problems with?
   a. Comprehending oral instructions
   b. Giving instructions to her peers
   c. Accurately interpreting facial expressions
   d. Learning classroom routines

Mathematics

31. Which answer choice is the most appropriate sequence for planning instructional units?
   a. Imaginary numbers → Square roots
   b. Rational numbers → Integers
   c. Integers → Rational numbers
   d. Real numbers → Square roots

- 9 -

32. Which number comes next in the sequence? *16, 24, 34, 46, 60*
    a. 72
    b. 74
    c. 76
    d. 56

33. Given that *x, y,* and *z* are non-zero integers, which expression must yield a rational number?
    a. $y\pi$

    b. $\sqrt{xy}$

    c. $\frac{x}{2y}$

    d. $\frac{\sqrt{2}}{x}$

34. Charlie recently took a standardized test. There were 65 people taking the test with Charlie; four of them earned higher scores than he did. Charlie falls into which score percentile?
    a. 99th
    b. 97th
    c. 95th
    d. 93rd

35. When given the equation 8B + 11= 43, a student found B = 6.75. What mistake did the student most likely make?
    a. When isolating the like terms, the student divided incorrectly by 8.
    b. When isolating like terms, the student added instead of subtracting 11 from the right side.
    c. The student used the wrong order of operations.
    d. The student forgot to isolate like terms.

36. Use the information below to answer the question that follows.

½ =    ¾=   ⅝=

Which of the following equals 1?

a.

   +   +

b.

   -      +

c.

   +   -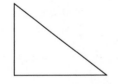

d.

   x   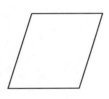   +

- 11 -

37. A child sells cups of lemonade for one quarter each. Which linear function best models the profits of the lemonade stand?

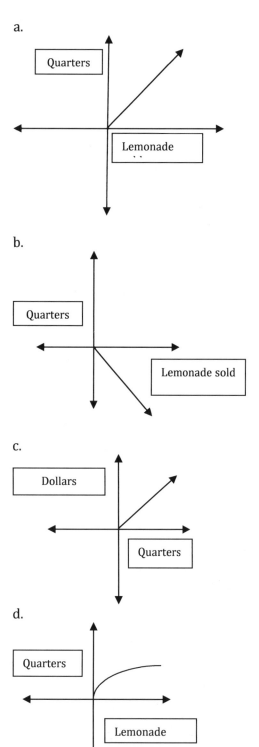

a.

Quarters

Lemonade

b.

Quarters

Lemonade sold

c.

Dollars

Quarters

d.

Quarters

Lemonade

38. Which function would not contain an X-intercept?

    a. $f(x) = (x + 3)^2$
    b. $f(x) = (x - 6)^2 - 2x+4$
    c. $f(x) = x^2 + 3$
    d. $f(x) = x^2 - 3x + 2$

39. Determine the coordinates of the next two points on the line.

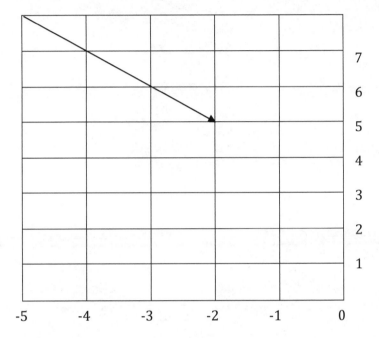

    a. (-3, 6), (-2, 5)
    b. (-1, 4), (0, 3)
    c. (4, -1), (2, -2)
    d. (3, 0), (2, -1)

40. What information is needed to determine that θ = 80°?

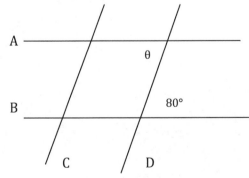

    a. That line B is perpendicular to line D.
    b. That line A is perpendicular to line C.
    c. That lines C and D are parallel.
    d. That lines A and B are parallel.

41. Given the right triangle below, where ∠A = 60°, which expression represents the length of side BC?

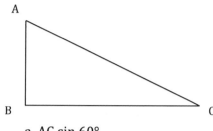

    a. AC sin 60°
    b. cos 60°
    c. AB sin 60°
    d. cos 30°

42. By the end of what grade level should a student be able to use algebraic principles to analyze both proportional and non-proportional linear relationships?
    a. 5th grade
    b. 6th grade
    c. 7th grade
    d. 8th grade

43. A family is considering building a wall from the back of their garage to their house. The two buildings already meet at one end and the resulting garden area would be in the shape of a right triangle. If the length of the wall is $\sqrt{369}$, and the long side of the garage is 12ft long, what is the area of the new garden in square feet?

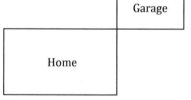

    a. 120
    b. 110
    c. 100
    d. 90

44. One gallon of paint covers 25ft^2 of wall. The painter has painted 2/5 of the wall. If the paint costs $6.25 per gallon, the painter must spend at least how much more to finish the wall?
    a. $18.75
    b. 56.25
    c. $12.50
    d. $15.00

45. Which of the following statements is false regarding teaching mathematics to English-language learners?
    a. English-language learners often benefit from using manipulatives or other tangible tools to help them understand math concepts.
    b. English-language learners typically find it much easier to participate in English-speaking mathematics classes, since they are usually less dependent on language than other subjects.
    c. Teachers should place students into small groups or pairs when possible so that they feel comfortable asking questions and seeking further information needed to make progress.
    d. It is helpful to include math vocabulary in instruction so that all students, especially English-language learners, understand what specific words mean when discussing math concepts.

46. When planning a unit on linear equations, a teacher would most likely include discussion on which of the following topics?
    a. Conjugating to remove irrational denominators
    b. Gradient of a straight line
    c. Order of operations
    d. Characteristics of the diagonals of various quadrilaterals

47. A track runner recorded times for his sprint of 33, 27, 29, 30, and 34 seconds. Which expression represents the standard deviation of his recorded times?

a. $\dfrac{2.4^2+(-3.6)^2+(-1.6)^2+(-0.6)^2+3.4^2}{5}$

b. $\sqrt{\dfrac{2.4^2+(-3.6)^2+(-1.6)^2+(-0.6)^2+3.4^2}{5}}$

c. $\sqrt{\dfrac{2.4+(-3.6)+(-1.6)+(-0.6)+3.4}{5}}$

d. $\dfrac{2.4-3.6-1.6-0.6+3.4}{5}$

48. Out of 60 contestants, Matt was the 37th person disqualified from the spelling bee. In which quartile did he place?
    a. 1st
    b. 2nd
    c. 3rd
    d. 4th

49. Identify the correct prime factorization of 72.
    a. $2^3 \times 3^2$
    b. $3^2 \times 2^3$
    c. 8×9
    d. 12×6

50. Use the function y = 3x – 1 to determine the numbers that complete the function table.

X	2	4	
Y	5		17

a. x = 1, y = 8
b. x = 3, y = 10
c. x = 5, y = 12
d. x = 6, y = 11

51. Ms. Grimes knows that her 4th-grade students will be taking standardized tests next month and hopes to prepare them well. She notices during practice testing that the students are struggling with money concepts, particularly the concept of making change. This is not a complete surprise to her, based upon the students' class work. What would be the best way to approach this scenario?
    a. Review each question on the practice tests carefully and walk the students through the proper way to do each problem. Deliver the practice test again a few days later to determine if the students' skills have improved.
    b. Use test questions and answers from last year's test to practice and memorize
    c. Set up a miniature grocery store with real items and packages labeled with prices; allow the students to practice purchasing items at the "store" and making change. Monitor and review practice test questions.
    d. Give more lessons on, and review about, adding and subtracting decimals in order to help the students solidify their procedural knowledge. Explain that money concepts are simply word problems that involve decimals.

52. Ms. Byrne stresses the importance of daily math homework with her sixth- and seventh-grade students. She states that the consistent practice will help students solidify their understanding of mathematical principles. Ms. Byrne also reviews this homework on a daily basis to help her understand what the students understand and to guide her instruction. This practice is an example of:
    a. Summative assessment
    b. Diversity in assignments
    c. Formative assessment
    d. Standards set forth for middle-grade mathematics

53. Identify the steps that you would complete in the correct order to solve the following problem. Donna's monthly income is $2,200. She spends 0.1 of it on transportation, 0.3 of it on her house, 0.2 of it on food, and 0.15 of it on other things. If she saves the rest of her income, how much money can she save in ⅓ of a year?
    a. Add 0.1, 0.3, 0.2 and 0.15. Subtract this sum from $2,200. Divide the difference by 3.
    b. Divide $2,200 by 3. Add 0.1, 0.3, 0.2 and 0.15. Multiply this sum by the quotient of $2,200 divided by 3.
    c. Find the sum of 0.1, 0.3, 0.2 and 0.15. Multiply this sum by $2,200. Subtract this product from $2200. Multiply the difference by 4.
    d. Find the sum of 0.1, 0.3, 0.2 and 0.15. Multiply this sum by $2,200. Divide this product by 3. Subtract the quotient from $2,200.

54. The following table shows admission prices to a museum exhibit for members and non-members.

	Members	Non-Members
Adults	$8.50	$10.50
Sr. Citizens	$6.50	$8.50
Children	$5.50	$7.50

A family, made up of 4 adults who are members, 2 senior citizens who are members, 1 senior citizen who is not a member, 3 children who are members and 3 children who are not members, visited the exhibit. Find the total amount they paid for admission.
    a. $78.00
    b. $86.50
    c . $94.50
    d. $102.50

55. Ashley and Catherine departed to travel from town A to town B at constant speeds of 58 miles per hour and 63 miles per hour respectively, at the same time. How far apart were they after 3 ½ hours?
    a. 9 miles
    b. 15 miles
    c. 17 miles
    d. 17.5 miles

56. A square and a rectangle have the same area. If the rectangle has a length of 25 inches and a perimeter of 58 inches, find the length of one side of the square.
    a. 10 inches
    b. 10 square inches
    c. 100 inches
    d. 100 square inches

57. Mrs. Tucker has 75 smiley-face and 10 star stickers on her desk. If she gives away one-third of the smiley-face stickers, which diagram best represents the ratio of smiley-face to star stickers that she now has?

a.

b.

c.

d.

58. Which conclusion cannot be drawn from the student's score report?
   a. The student performed in the eighty-third percentile on the Language Expression section of the test.
   b. The student enjoys reading.
   c. The student's strongest area is Math Computation.
   d. The student's weakest area is Study Skills.

59. In a pack of 20 jelly beans, there are two licorice- and four cinnamon-flavored jelly beans. What is the probability of choosing a licorice jelly bean followed by a cinnamon jelly bean?

   a. $\frac{2}{5}$

   b. $\frac{8}{20}$

   c. $\frac{2}{95}$

   d. $\frac{1}{50}$

60. A sheriff's office in a small town creates a chart of violent crimes in the area for the previous year. Based on the chart below, which prediction for the following year seems the most appropriate?

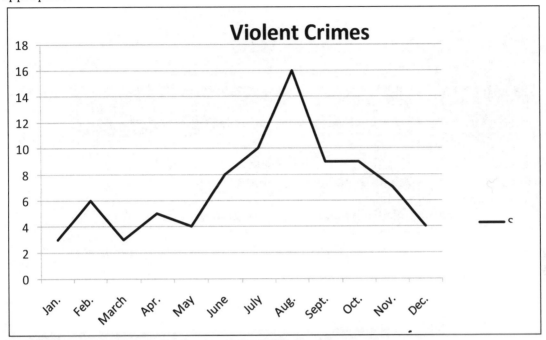

a. The winter months are likely to see a spike in violent crime rates.
b. Holiday months will likely see an increase in personal theft.
c. Violent crimes will be greatest when the weather is the warmest.
d. The number of violent crimes per month will continue to grow throughout the year.

History/Social Studies

61. European explorers were responsible for the following changes in the lives of Native Americans, except:
a. The proliferation of horses and guns in the region.
b. The introduction of new diseases amongst the Native American population.
c. The strengthening of bonds between all Native American groups in response to European aggression.
d. The expansion of Christian mission work.

62. During a report on the Industrial Revolution, Mary uses a poster to illustrate cause and effect relationships in the War of 1812. What could be added to make the organizer more informative?

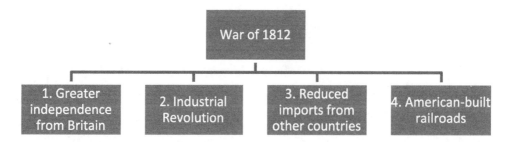

    a. Placing boxes 1, 3 and 4 below box 2 and adding details to support
    b. A third tier that provides details about boxes 1, 2 and 3
    c. Handouts for each student to take home
    d. Music, video or other multimedia to make the presentation more interesting

63. The concept of Manifest Destiny relates most closely to which era in American history?
    a. Cold War
    b. Civil Rights
    c. Gilded Age
    d. Westward Expansion

64. Ms. Bailey's students have been studying the American Civil Rights Movement. Which country should she use for a parallel study to help students understand similarities and differences between cultures?
    a. South Africa
    b. England
    c. Morocco
    d. China

65. Although Roosevelt's New Deal solved many problems, it:
    a. failed to provide direct relief to the poor.
    b. had little effect on the problem of unemployment.
    c. raised the national debt.
    d. weakened labor unions.

66. A 6th-grade English class will begin to read *Sadako and the Thousand Paper Cranes*, a novel about a young Japanese woman who refuses to give up hope while ill with leukemia, a result of an atom bomb that fell on her city. Which of the following choices would complement this novel most effectively?
    a. Discussion of leukemia's effects on the body.
    b. A visit to a museum to view photographs of the aftermath of Hiroshima and Nagasaki.
    c. Selected text on Japanese culture and how it has been affected by the Second World War.
    d. An origami lesson in which students can fold their own paper cranes just as the protagonist does.

67. Put the following events in order from oldest to most recent.
1) Martin Luther King led the March on Washington.
2) Brown v. Board of Education overturned the policy of "separate but equal" education.
3) The Student Non-Violent Coordinating Committee began staging sit-ins at segregated lunch counters in the South.
4) The arrest of Rosa Parks sparked the Montgomery Bus Boycott.
    a. 2,4,3,1
    b. 1,3,2,4
    c. 3,4,1,2
    d. 2,1,4,3

68. In the social sciences, the term "prehistory" refers to...
    a. The period before humans inhabited the Earth
    b. The period before the fall of the Roman Empire
    c. The period before history was recorded in writing
    d. The period prior to the formation of the Earth

69. How did the Crusader army that went on the First Crusade differ from the Crusader armies that Pope Urban II envisioned?
    a. There was no difference. The people of Europe were accustomed to obeying clerical direction and eagerly joined the cause creating an army that was primarily made up of faithful Christians from all social classes led by a select group of knights who were responsible for leading and training their armies.
    b. There was no difference. The people of Europe obeyed clerical direction and stayed home to pray for the success of an army composed entirely of knights and professional other military personnel.
    c. Pope Urban II had envisioned an army of skilled knights and professional soldiers; instead, men and women from all classes joined together to retake the Holy Land.
    d. Pope Urban II had envisioned an army composed of faithful Christians of from all social classes led by a group of select knights; instead the army was primarily made up of knights and other professional military personnel.

70. Who was Genghis Khan?
    a. The founder of the Mongol Empire
    b. The leader of the Hunnic Empire in the 5th Century who led his people to attack into Western Europe.
    c. The leader of the 19th Century Taiping Rebellion
    d. None of the above

71. Mecca is an important site for Muslims primarily because:
    a. it is the birthplace of the prophet Muhammad.
    b. according to the Koran, the Second Coming will occur in Mecca.
    c. Muhammad fled to Mecca from Medina in 622 A.D,
    d. it is home of the Ka'ba, a holy structure said to be built by Abraham.

72. Which of these was NOT an immediate consequence of the Age of Exploration?
    a. the development of more accurate navigation instruments
    b. the introduction of new foods and other goods to Europe
    c. the decline of England as a world power
    d. the discovery of new lands where people might seek a better life

73. What method did Johannes Gutenberg use to create printing plates for his printing press?
   a. Woodcuts – he had a team of apprentices carve each page out of wood plates.
   b. Metal etchings – the letters were etched into specially treated metal plates which were then placed in special acid baths to create printing plates.
   c. Moveable clay type – Gutenberg carved moveable type out of clay and would press the letters into hot wax tablets to create printing plates.
   d. Moveable type – Gutenberg cast metal type through the use of molds in order to achieve the individual letters which were then loaded into composing sticks, which were then used to form printing plates.

74. Which of the following choices details a benefit derived from widespread internet use paired with a corresponding negative consequence?
   a. Greater access to information; decreased certainty regarding accuracy and validity of said information.
   b. Social networking capacity; connectedness to friends and families.
   c. Higher vulnerability to identity theft; increased opportunities for research and inquiry.
   d. Higher rates of intellectual ability among children and teens; decrease in after-school jobs performed for compensation.

75. Which statement most closely illustrates the philosophy of integrated studies?
   a. Teachers should be familiar with all academic disciplines and skills, rather than specializing in one area in-depth.
   b. Each student must have equal access to any and all opportunities within the Texas public school system at large.
   c. All aspects of Social Studies, and in fact other academic disciplines, are interrelated and evolve simultaneously in a complex manner.
   d. Each skill set within the Social Studies discipline should be separately identified and taught as stand-alone sub-disciplines to increase clarity and understanding in all students.

76. How could a teacher with 4th and 5th grade students put the concept of citizenship into a relevant context for her students?
   a. Invite prominent citizens from the community to visit the class and speak about what citizenship means to the individual and the group.
   b. Create a class "community" in which all students have jobs in the classroom and vote on issues important to the group.
   c. Agree upon a class-wide service project through which students can help other in need.
   d. Assign an essay topic requiring each student to write about "What Citizenship Means to Me."

77. Which of the following choices best defines the concept of judicial review?
   a. A quarterly journal containing articles and essays on current legal issues.
   b. The process of reviewing evidence in a court case.
   c. The court's power to decide if a law is constitutional.
   d. The censoring of a judicial figure, specifically courtroom judges.

78. In Government class, students are reading about and discussing controversy around immigration and naturalization laws. Which of the following Supreme Court decisions is ideal for illustrating the United States' long history of dialogue about citizeznship?
    a. Dred Scott v Sandford, 1857
    b. Roe v Wade, 1973
    c. Miranda v Arizona, 1963
    d. Marbury *v Madison, 1803*

79. If you know the longitude of a city in the United States, you can determine:
    a. the state in which it is located.
    b. the time zone in which it is located.
    c. exactly how far it is from the equator.
    d. approximate average winter temperature.

Use the map below to answer questions 80 and 81:

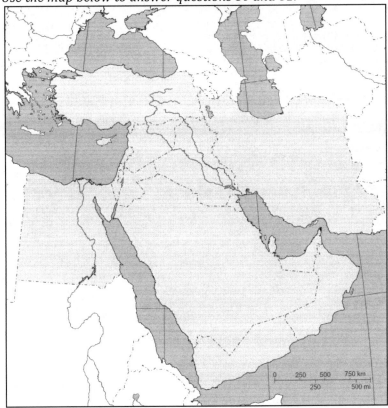

80. The map above depicts what area, specifically?
    a. The place of origin for all major world religions.
    b. The Holy Land
    c. The Middle East
    d. The Strait of Gibraltar

81. A group of 7th- and 8th-graders have elected to do research projects on the relationship and common interests between their state and the Middle East Region. What information could be added to this map to assist the students?
   a. Commerce and Industry
   b. Political divisions
   c. Religious representations
   d. An inset depicting the southwestern United States

82. A nation that is NOT a member of NAFTA is:
   a. Mexico.
   b. Brazil.
   c. the United States.
   d. Canada.

83. The physical geography of a region most directly affects:
   a. the religious beliefs of the native population.
   b. the family structure of the native population.
   c. the dietary preferences of the native population.
   d. the language spoken by the native population.

84. The following illustration in the students' textbook is an example of what kind of industry?

   a. Primary
   b. Secondary
   c. Tertiary
   d. Healthcare

85. A downturn in economic activity, defined by a lowered Gross Domestic Product for two or more consecutive quarters, constitutes a:
   a. Depression
   b. Government Rescue Plan
   c. Recession
   d. Global Economic Crisis

86. One reason for Jefferson's opposition to the Bank of the United States was that he:
    a. did not think the Bank would effectively further his goal of establishing a strong central government.
    b. was a strict constructionist.
    c. believed the Bank would give an unfair advantage to the southern states.
    d. distrusted the fiscal policies of the Democratic-Republicans.

87. The main reason that the Federal Reserve Board lowers interest rates is to:
    a. lower prices.
    b. stimulate consumer spending.
    c. encourage international trade.
    d. control inflation.

88. A teacher is planning a "Social Sciences Career Week." Parents of her students will visit in order to speak with the class about possibilities for career choices after graduation. Which of the following could be listed for Wednesday?

Career Week, April 26-30
Monday: Psychologist, Billie Summers
Tuesday: Criminologist, Katherine Walters
Wednesday: TBAThursday: Linguist, Todd Snape
Friday: Political Science Professor, Ben Thomas

    a. Biologist, Maureen Benedict
    b. Entymologist, James Frank
    c. Anthropologist, Asher Vance
    d. Physicist, Amy Van Buren

Use the chart below to answer question 89.

Area	April 1, 2000	April 1, 1990	State Rank as of April 1, 2000	State Rank as of April 1, 1990
Alabama	4,447,100	4,040,587	23	22
Alaska	626,932	550,043	48	49
Arizona	5,130,632	3,665,228	20	24
Arkansas	2,673,400	2,350,725	33	33
California	33,871,648	29,760,021	1	1
Colorado	4,301,261	3,294,394	24	26
Connecticut	3,405,565	3,287,116	29	27
Delaware	783,600	666,168	45	46
District of Columbia	572,059	606,900	(NA)	(NA)
Florida	15,982,378	12,937,926	4	4
Georgia	8,186,453	6,478,216	10	11
Hawaii	1,211,537	1,108,229	42	41
Idaho	1,293,953	1,006,749	39	42
Illinois	12,419,293	11,430,602	5	6
Indiana	6,080,485	5,544,159	14	14
Iowa	2,926,324	2,776,755	30	30
Kansas	2,688,418	2,477,574	32	32
Kentucky	4,041,769	3,685,296	25	23
Louisiana	4,468,976	4,219,973	22	21
Maine	1,274,923	1,227,928	40	38
Maryland	5,296,486	4,781,468	19	19
Massachusetts	6,349,097	6,016,425	13	13
Michigan	9,938,444	9,295,297	8	8
Minnesota	4,919,479	4,375,099	21	20
Mississippi	2,844,658	2,573,216	31	31
Missouri	5,595,211	5,117,073	17	15
Montana	902,195	799,065	44	44
Nebraska	1,711,263	1,578,385	38	36
Nevada	1,998,257	1,201,833	35	39
New Hampshire	1,235,786	1,109,252	41	40
New Jersey	8,414,350	7,730,188	9	9
New Mexico	1,819,046	1,515,069	36	37
New York	18,976,457	17,990,455	3	2
North Carolina	8,049,313	6,628,637	11	10
North Dakota	642,200	638,800	47	47
Ohio	11,353,140	10,847,115	7	7
Oklahoma	3,450,654	3,145,585	27	28
Oregon	3,421,399	2,842,321	28	29
Pennsylvania	12,281,054	11,881,643	6	5
Rhode Island	1,048,319	1,003,464	43	43
South Carolina	4,012,012	3,486,703	26	25
South Dakota	754,844	696,004	46	45
Tennessee	5,689,283	4,877,185	16	17
Texas	20,851,820	16,986,510	2	3
Utah	2,233,169	1,722,850	34	35
Vermont	608,827	562,758	49	48
Virginia	7,078,515	6,187,358	12	12
Washington	5,894,121	4,866,692	15	18
West Virginia	1,808,344	1,793,477	37	34
Wisconsin	5,363,675	4,891,769	18	16
Wyoming	493,782	453,588	50	50

89. Consider the chart above, listing states ranked by population data. Of those states whose populations increased between 1990 and 2000, which state would have shown a decrease in population had another census been taken in 2006?
    a. Missouri
    b. Wyoming
    c. New York
    d. Louisiana

- 26 -

Use the information below to answer question 90.

> My name is Amorosa. I am fourteen years old and I live near the Gulf Coast in South Texas. My father runs an oil refinery and my mother is a schoolteacher. I have two brothers, named Jorge and Emil—they are sixteen-year-old twins! After school, when there is no soccer practice, I love to spend time in the Art classroom. I love the paints, clays, fabrics, and other materials used to create beautiful things. Next year, my family and friends will celebrate my *Quinceañera*, a large party in honor of my 15th birthday. There will be music, food, a Court of Honor made up of my friends, and most importantly, a beautiful dress. In my city, there are talented women who design and make ball gowns that we will wear. When I celebrate my *Quinceañera*, I will help the dress designer create my dress.

90. How could Amorosa's teacher encourage her to use her interests to build her understanding of various cultural influences and diversity?

    a. Ask Amorosa to bring in pictures of all of the events surrounding the celebration to show her classmates.

    b. Encourage Amorosa to research similar customs in other cultures present in Texas (e.g., Swiss, French, Native American) and compare and contrast them.

    c. Require Amorosa to speak to her class about what her family's heritage means to her and how her culture has influenced the person she has become.

    d. Allow Amorosa to use her artistic skills to teach so that she can work with children of all ages and backgrounds.

Science

91. All of the following are membrane-bound organelles except

    a. Nucleoli

    b. Chromoplasts

    c. Mitochondria

    d. Endoplasmic reticulum

92. The illustration below depicts the structures of glucose (top) and sucrose (bottom). The body converts which kind of sugar to energy?

    a. Sucrose

    b. Fructose

    c. Glucose

    d. Dextrose

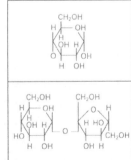

93. A teacher provides her students with the checklist shown below for homework. What is the most likely purpose of the activity?

	Me	Parent 1	Parent 2
Eye color			
Ability to roll tongue			
Presence of widow's peak			
Hand dominance			
Presence of dimples			

   a. To illustrate the purpose of taking medical history in the event of illness on a smaller, less negative scale.
   b. To demonstrate how genetics plays a role in determining what traits are passed through generations.
   c. To help students feel connected to parents during a tumultuous social period by identifying basic similarities.
   d. To show the process of Darwin's theories of natural selection in humans.

94. Which of the following statements outlines an historical and fundamental basis for the ethics of animal vivisection (dissection) in a middle-school biology class?
   a. Students should understand what they consume each day and how their food affects their bodies.
   b. Dissection helps students determine whether or not they want to pursue scientific research related to investigation of bodily systems.
   c. By participating in dissection, students receive a hands-on learning experience that deepens their understanding of anatomy, physiology, and life processes.
   d. There is no ethical basis for the dissection of animals in classrooms. This practice harms both animal species and participating students.

95. The human eye perceives leaves on a tree as green because of light that is
   a. Absorbed
   b. Refracted
   c. Reflected
   d. Diffracted

96. After their field trip, the students decide to work on a project together. Which of the following would be the best project, if its purpose were to protect biodiversity in its community?
   a. Working together to improve the quality of food at the zoo.
   b. Beginning a campaign to ban gas-motored boats from the pond.
   c. Exploring water-treatment methods that are non-toxic.
   d. Starting a recycling drive at school.

97. A 7th-grade class is currently studying *biodiversity*. The class will be taking a field trip to help deepen their conceptual understanding of this concept. Students will also have a chance to practice working with and recording in their new field journals, which they will be using for the next few months. Where is the most likely destination for their field trip?
    a. The zoo
    b. The local pond
    c. The water processing plant
    d. The recycling center

98. In highly industrialized areas, trees used to become covered in soot. Eventually, most moths found in that area were gray rather than white. Which factor most likely contributed to the change in color of these moths?
    a. Natural selection
    b. Genetic drift
    c. Sexual selection
    d. Punctuated equilibrium

99. The horn of a rhinoceros and human hair are evolutionarily related. They are
    a. Ancestral characteristics
    b. Detrimental characteristics
    c. Homologous characteristics
    d. Analogous characteristics

100. Which of the following is NOT a useful source of evidence with respect to the evolutionary history of an organism?
    a. Its placement in the fossil record
    b. Its anatomy
    c. Its distribution among the continents
    d. Its population size

101. The primary chemical process in the sun that creates light is
    a. The fission of helium into hydrogen
    b. The fission of lithium into helium and hydrogen
    c. The fusion of hydrogen into helium
    d. The fusion of helium into beryllium

102. The factor most responsible for determining which season an area is experiencing is
    a. Elevation
    b. The position of the earth in its orbit around the sun
    c. Latitude
    d. Air masses

103. The illustration below depicts the rock cycle. This cycle illustrates the fact that rocks are not unchanging entities; they undergo changes over time. Which of the following would not be considered a force driving the rock cycle?

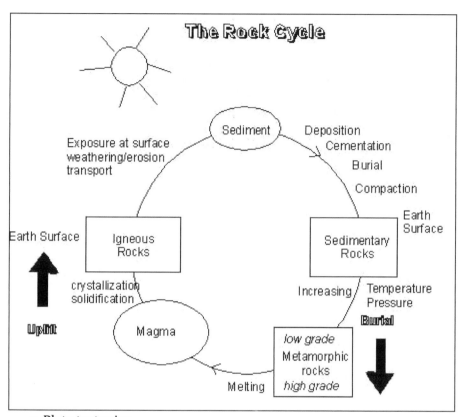

a. Plate tectonics
b. The water cycle
c. Global warming
d. Volcanic eruptions

104. Which of the following is a true statement about a caldera?
    a. It is formed when a massive explosion destroys the cone of a volcano.
    b. It is created when the rock above a fault plane moves up relative to the rock below.
    c. It is a class of volcano characterized by quiet eruptions.
    d. It is formed by cooling lava.

105. Which of the following is NOT a significant factor in the dramatic increase of the human population over the past few hundred years?
    a. Increased availability of habitable land
    b. Scientific advances in agriculture
    c. Improved sanitation
    d. An understanding of the causes of communicable diseases

106. Which of the following scenarios best describes a lesson in which a teacher has utilized *anchored instruction* applied to space science?
    a. Students work with solar system trading cards, matching parts of the solar system based upon characteristics and traits.
    b. A teacher gives a lecture regarding the traits of each planet in our solar system, followed by group discussion.
    c. Students do background reading on the size and scope of the solar system and use a scale-model of the system to answer questions about planet sizes and distance.
    d. Students participate in an experiment that allows them to make their own miniature Black Holes in class, observing and recording behaviors.

107. Which step in the hydrologic cycle, if absent, would directly result in the effects of global warming?
    a. Transpiration
    b. Radiation
    c. Condensation
    d. Oceanic evaporation

108. On the ocean floor, volcanoes can erupt, causing what are known as thermal vents. Temperatures can be very high near these vents. Which of the following types of organisms would most likely live near them?
    a. Protists
    b. Eukaryotes
    c. Prokaryotes
    d. Metazoans

109. The percentage of the earth's water that is saline most closely matches which figure?
    a. 98%
    b. 70%
    c. 30%
    d. 2%

110. The British Isles on the east side of the Atlantic Ocean are often warmer than the coastal parts of Canada at the same latitude. This is because ocean currents warm the atmosphere of the British Isles. This kind of heat transfer is called
    a. Radiation
    b. Convection
    c. Thermoregulation
    d. Transduction

111. Which of the following is a constant?
    a. The freezing point of water
    b. The temperature at which iron ore will melt
    c. The human population size
    d. The time the sun rises each day

112. Ms. Burke plans to illustrate the difference between physical and chemical changes in substances. Which experiment can the students perform that will allow the students to observe a chemical change?

    a. The students place an ice cube in a bowl and allow it to melt. They can then place the dish into the freezer, causing it to re-form into another shape.

    b. A variety of objects, including metal nails, are left on the windowsill outside of the classroom for a period of time. Students observe and document the changes, including rust forming on the nails.

    c. Students observe and record evaporation rates of water from various kinds of receptacles.

    d. A food preparation area allows students to create their own snacks. While preparing the food, students observe the spreading of cream cheese on crackers, the melting of butter onto bread, and milk being added to cereals.

113. Which of the following compounds is not allowed in a school laboratory because it is a potential carcinogen?

    a. Lead

    b. Benzene

    c. Aspartame

    d. Methanol

114. Which of the following is NOT an example of one of Newton's laws of motion at work?

    a. Once in orbit, a satellite will continue moving around the earth.

    b. It takes three times as much force to move a block that has twice the mass of another.

    c. A ball rolling across the floor will continue moving across the floor.

    d. When a shotgun is fired, the gun moves sharply in the opposite direction of the bullet.

115. In an experiment, you want to measure the amount of mass a piece of wood liberates when it burns. The most accurate way of doing this would be to

    a. Measure the volume and pressure of the gases emitted by the burning wood, and then calculate the number of molecules present.

    b. Chill the gases emitted by the burning wood over liquid nitrogen so the mass of the solid carbon dioxide (dry ice) can be measured.

    c. Determine the mass of the ash after the wood burns.

    d. Measure the mass of the wood before and after it burns.

116. A teacher posts large, colored pictures of various items around her 4th-grade classroom, including a bicycle, an airplane, an electric scooter, a skateboard and a tractor. What might be her lesson for today?

    a. Alternate modes of personal transportation in the absence of a car or truck

    b. A discussion of which objects need to burn fuel, use electricity, or need other forms of power to move

    c. The aerodynamic design and how it affects movement

    d. Collection of data regarding students' experience with various vehicles and analysis of the data

117. What class of material increases in conductivity with increased vibrational motion within the material?
    a. LASERS
    b. MASERS
    c. photoelectric sensors
    d. semiconductors

118. What wave characteristic determines if electromagnetic radiation is in the form of a radio wave or an X-ray?
    a. frequency
    b. amplitude
    c. wavelength
    d. speed of light

119. What wave characteristic is related to the pitch of a sound?
    a. frequency
    b. amplitude
    c. wavelength
    d. speed of sound

120. Which of the following would have the *most* massive radioactive decay?
    a. an alpha particle
    b. a beta ray
    c. gamma rays
    d. x-rays

Answers and Explanations

Literature and Language Studies

1. B: The words in the boxes suggest that the box on the left is the "cause" and the one on the right is the "effect." The arrow in the middle shows the relationship between the cause and the effect; the boxes and arrow can even be reversed if it is easier for students to discuss the effect first and the cause next. In choices A and D, the arrow would not apply to the concepts. Because choice C contains two ideas, it could be mistaken for the correct answer. However, there is little to no causation or causal relationship between the two ideas—they are two separate but equal analytical tools often used simultaneously.

2. C: Phonemic awareness is the understanding that words are composed of individual sounds, and phonics is the practice of connecting these sounds to their written counterparts. If a student cannot hear the individual sounds that comprise words, then he or she will not be able to link those sounds with the written letters that represent them.

3. B: A words correct per minute test would most likely be used by a reading teacher to conduct a preliminary screening of a student's reading fluency. Reading fluency is the ability to quickly decode words. Students who can read fluently are able to pay much more attention to higher-order aspects of the text, which leads to increased comprehension.

4. A: The author's intent is what distinguishes narrative text from expository text. Narrative texts are written primarily to entertain, while the main purpose of expository *texts is to inform readers. Both types of texts can vary greatly in length, level of difficulty, and type of vocabulary used.

5. D: In general, poems are divided into stanzas, or smaller units within the poem. Sonnets and haiku are both types of poems, and iambic pentameter is a type of meter within a poem.

6. C: Such an image paired with an article about globalization would be intended to emphasize the way in which globalization has exacerbated economic inequality in many parts of the world. Capturing two contrasting symbols within the same image is a common technique in journalistic photography. Such juxtapositions are intended to arouse emotion and, in some cases, a sense of irony in the observer.

7. D: Literacy skills include reading, writing, comprehending, expressing, communicating and a whole host of other concepts. Often, an individual student will possess varying abilities within each aspect of their literacy development. A teacher should take care not to approach this kind of student with an inflexible plan, or with the notion that certain skills (such as fluency) must be fully developed before others (such as comprehension). Setting small goals with the individual student allows him to take ownership over the process and work on various skill sets in tandem. All components of each student's literacy can improve simultaneously.

8. B: The term "instructional level" refers to the level at which a child can work on building reading fluency without the text being too easy or too difficult. If the child can read approximately 90% of the words without assistance, the text will be considered "instructional level." If the student needs less help, the teacher should move him to a more challenging-to-read piece or consider the text to be "independent level" reading. If the piece is too difficult, the level of difficulty should be lowered, or extra help should be provided in the areas of difficulty.

9. B: Students build vocabulary and word knowledge through exposure and are more likely to remember words in context. The best way to help a student learn more words is through giving what they are learning a context for memory. Introducing a variety of reading material gives students more exposure to different kinds of words. Another way to introduce vocabulary is to encourage students to engage in conversation with adults; Students will be more likely to build sight words and vocabulary if they are not focused on learning words for the sake of learning them; rather, the words are retained easily if the student can remember how he or she learned it.

10. C: Non-fiction writing can cover a multitude of styles and content. The pieces Mr. Blankenship plans to introduce are not specified in the question, and could be anything from newspaper articles to biographies. Teaching students to preview the topic and information will help them attend to main ideas and important details. The summarizing step helps students put relevant ideas together and categorize information in their minds. Because non-fiction text is often more detailed than conceptual, choice B creates a three-step process that will help students understand and retain the ideas which they have read.

11. B: Emergent readers are students who are beginning to show signs of reading and writing independently, but still require quite a bit of scaffolding in their work. Often, these readers will show varied abilities within each of the components of literacy, perhaps working independently in one area while needing more help in another. Therefore, emergent readers benefit from specific instruction and exercises that address all the areas of literacy, rather than focusing on one skill at a time. In this way, all of their skills can evolve simultaneously and, ideally, more quickly.

12. C: Failing to remember previously-learned concepts is a red flag suggesting a learning disability. Note that the student is failing to remember concepts he has already *learned*, and not simply ideas that have been *introduced* once. If a student seems to know something one day and then does not know it the next, there may be a learning disability. The girls in the first two choices do not warrant special instruction; rather, they exhibit areas for improvement that can be worked on inside their normal classrooms, as part of daily instruction. Billy, in choice D, likely has some motivation or skill deficits in relation to writing that can be addressed in partnership with him, inside of daily lessons.

13. B: Reading fluency refers to the speed, accuracy and appropriate intonation with which an individual reads. As a student is beginning to learn to read, he or she will be working primarily on sounding out words (phonetics), building recognition of words (sight words), and reading with speed and appropriate vocal modulation (emotion and pauses for punctuation). A fluent reader will read at a natural pace without making many mistakes. He or she will typically pause appropriately to communicate punctuation and modulate the voice with expression to add interest to the text. Comprehension (choice B) is typically thought of as a reading concept that evolves in tandem with fluency, but the former is not a component of the latter.

14. A: It is important for students who are continuing to practice their reading skills to work at the appropriate level of challenge. Grade levels can be subjective when it comes to reading skills; i.e., not all 5th-grade texts contain the same material or skill levels. Students are not always best at choosing books that are challenging for them, sometimes opting for material that is too easy or too difficult. If the student can read the majority of the words in the book, but still find few new words to challenge them, the book is likely at an appropriate level of challenge.

15. D: Students' final drafts should be held to higher grammatical standards than their informal speeches or their early drafts. Informal speech and rough drafts are both initial attempts at communication, and there should be allowances for mistakes at this stage as students experiment with new ideas, vocabulary words, and sentence structures. In addition, standards for grammatical correctness and precision are generally lower for informal speech than for writing, largely because of the role that nonverbal communication plays in informal conversation. Because formal writing lacks the benefit of nonverbal communication, greater precision and richness of vocabulary are required for successful communication to occur.

16. B: It is true that word analysis can be taught by explicitly modeling the thought process used to infer the meaning of a word. Word analysis encompasses the many strategies readers can use to identify the meanings of unfamiliar words. It is different from decoding, which refers to pronouncing the word phonetically.

17. D: Using oral language practice to improve students' vocabulary and reading comprehension skills is a common practice in many classrooms. Discussing a text aloud before reading it allows students to activate prior knowledge about the topic, connect vocabulary words that are part of their oral repertoire to the written words on the page, and gain additional information about the text through nonverbal cues provided by the teacher and other students.

18. C: When instructing an ESL student who is already literate in his native language, reading teachers should consider that there is significant diversity among the basic operating principles of written languages and that, as a result, there may be central principles of written English with which the student is unfamiliar. Because some world languages are not alphabetic, even a highly educated English language learner may struggle with the alphabetic principle of written English if it is not explicitly taught. However, the teacher should research the student's native language to gather this information rather than assuming that the student has no frame of reference for the alphabetic principle or the phonetic irregularities of written English.

19. B: The symptoms that Mrs. Cornelius has observed in her daughter suggest a weakness in reading fluency. The fact that Chloe can easily read individual words shows that decoding is not the problem, and the low level of reading comprehension she has demonstrated is most likely a result of Chloe's poor reading fluency.

20. A: When selecting texts for silent reading in the classroom, teachers should choose a range of texts, including some above and below grade level to accommodate students with varying ability levels. Also, providing a range of texts to accommodate all students will make silent reading more productive.

21. B: Folk tales are stories that have been passed down orally through generations, and typically contain a kind of moral or lesson. Folk tales are most appropriate in this case because they are so influenced and bear a strong relationship to oral traditions across all cultures that could be present in the classroom. This genre provides many opportunities not only to read aloud, but to discuss the importance or oral language in learning lessons about culture and behavior.

22. D: There will always be students who are quieter in class for a variety of reasons—they may be shy, be disinterested in the topics, or simply have trouble translating thoughts into verbal communication quickly enough. By reducing the number of contributors in the group, quieter students will have more time and freedom to speak aloud. Mr. Everly can then join the groups containing those students and observe them to ensure they are communicating appropriately and

have a thorough-enough grasp of the material. If he is unsure about how the student is progressing, he can also engage him in conversation in the group without singling out that particular student.

23. C: Students will not typically arrive in the classroom with excellent listening skills; these skills must be introduced and honed as any others would be. Students often benefit from previewing material or pointing out what they should be listening *for*, since it will be virtually impossible for them to retain every piece of information proffered during class time. If the information is previewed, they are predisposed to listen carefully to important topics. When asked questions about the information, the teacher will be able to monitor how well they listened, as well as whether they understood what they heard. Choice A does involve listening skills, but does not provide direct instruction or a method of monitoring improvement; choices B and D monitor improvement but do not build skills.

24. D: Listening is a vital part of being literate and communicative. Students must often listen to understand instructions and content in class, as well as to make sense of the world around them. From an early age, students learn to listen in order to hear stories and other kinds of literature. This listening practice helps them prepare to learn in other ways, such as through reading and viewing. However, once other literacy skills start to develop, students still benefit from honing their listening skills. This practice helps them communicate more effectively and utilize every part of their senses to take in information. Literature and other texts can be appreciated through listening just as much as through reading.

25. B: As the students strive to understand individuals from around the world, the project would not be complete without attention to that individual's mode of oral expression. In reading about and repeating the research subject's own words, the students will have an opportunity, if guided appropriately, to learn about how a person's speech reflects their identity and thoughts. The students will assume the role of a person very different from themselves and be able to place themselves into another perspective via oral language.

26. A: Graphemes are individual letters within a word, which can be distinguished from phonemes, or letter-sounds. The term syllable refers to a single unit of sound formed by a letter or combination of letters. The set of words in choice A holds words with more than a few letters, but only two to three syllables. Choice B consists of words with few graphemes and few syllables. Conversely, choice C holds words with both many graphemes and syllables. The final choice does not exhibit a pattern that is relevant to this question. This

27. D: Many students will rely too much on technology in the writing process, preventing them from making progress. The last choice uses a specific form of technology, an online program, to help the student organize ideas into an outline. This program keeps the student from skipping one of the most important aspects of learning to write: planning and organization. There are many tools that a student can use on a computer that will help him or her get ready to write. However, choice B shows how a computer or word processor can be used in an incorrect way. Choices A and C do not provide direct instruction on the writing process, but simply record ideas for the sake of retention.

28. A: While this answer may seem to be obvious, some teachers will make the mistake of allowing students to choose their own topics without help. However, a new researcher will likely need help choosing a topic that is appropriately narrow. Some students will choose topics from which they cannot possibly cover enough related information and produce a comprehensive report. Conversely, some students will choose an excessively narrow or obscure topic that will not provide enough material for research. There may also be topic choices that are not appropriate for a

particular student based upon age or maturity level. The teacher would do well to meet with students and guide them in choosing topics that will suit first-time researchers as they learn this process.

29. B: In this scenario, every student will engage in individual inquiry each week. The assignment gives students some freedom to investigate what is interesting or important to them and share that information with their peers. In this way, students will be exercising the exact process of independent research each week on a small scale. Choice A gives too much freedom, since students may simply be checking out books that are fun to read, thereby circumventing the whole process of research. Choice C is one way to incorporate research, but could draw the project out for so long that the students do not grasp its purpose. Choice C provides opportunities for students to research answers, but does not prevent students from opting not to do the research.

30. A: Students with receptive language disorders have difficulty translating written and spoken language into meaningful ideas. This makes it difficult for students to understand oral directions. Some students with receptive language disorders also have accompanying expressive language disorders, meaning that they struggle to translate everyday concepts into words. They may have difficulty giving instructions to others or learning classroom routines, but these outcomes are not direct results of the receptive language disorder.

Mathematics

31. C: Integers are defined as the set of natural numbers (including zero) and their negatives. You cannot define rational numbers without understanding integers. Rational numbers are defined as any number that can be expressed by a/b, when both a and b are integers, but b is not zero. Therefore an appropriate order for lesson planning would be to discuss integers before rational numbers. Imaginary numbers arise as a necessity in the study of square roots and should therefore not be studied before them. Real numbers are typically introduced with the study of square roots.

32. C: The numbers in this sequence progress according to a pattern. Each progressing number can be expressed by the equation x + 2 = n, where x = the difference between the previous two numbers and n = the number added to the previous number to yield the progressing number. For instance, the difference in 24 and 16 is 8. By adding 2 to 8, you know that you must add 10 to 24 in order to yield 34. In the next part of the sequence, x = 10 and n = 12. 34 + 12 = 46, the next number in the sequence.

33. C: A rational number is any number that can be expressed as a/b where a and b are both integers and b ≠ 0. Both x and y are integers and do not equal zero. Any integer multiplied by 2 will yield another integer. Choice C expresses an equation in which an integer is divided by another integer, which yields a rational number.

34. D: The formula for percentile is $n = \frac{N}{100}p + \frac{1}{2}$, where n is the rank in the total of all values of N. In this case the rank, n, equals 61 while the total number of values, N, is 65. Using these values for n and N, the closest correct answer is 93.

35. B: When learning to solve algebraic equations, it is necessary to treat the two sides of an equation equally. In order to isolate the variable, the first step is to subtract the constant from both sides. In this case, the constant is 11. By reworking the problem using the suggestion found in choice B, it is possible to arrive at the student's incorrect answer. The best method to solving this question is to use a trial and error method, determining which answer yields the incorrect answer.

36. D: Explanation: (3/4 x 1/2) + 5/8 = 3/8 + 5/8= 1
Triangle = 3/4; Rhombus = 1/2; Diamond = 5/8. Multiply 3/4 by 1/2 to get 3/8. Add 3/8 and 5/8 to get 8/8 which equals 1.

37. A: The relationship between lemonade sold and the amount of quarters varies directly. As one variable increases, so does the other. The function in choice B suggests that the child loses quarters for every cup of lemonade sold. Choice C is inaccurate in that it neglects to include the cups of lemonade in its measurement. Quarters and dollars do not increase at the same rate. Choice D is not a linear function and suggests that there is a limit to how much money the child can earn, no matter how much lemonade is sold.

38. C: In order to solve for the X-intercept of a function, set the function equal to zero and solve for x. When this is done for $f(x) = x^2 + 3$, there will be an imaginary value for x, therefore there is no X-intercept. When given the function $(x) = x^2 + c$, the constant C moves the original graph up or down depending on its value. The parabola graphed from $f(x) = x^2$, usually touching the point (0, 0) is moved up to point (0, C), or in this case, (0, 3).

39. B: (-1, 4), (0, 3) Explanation: The line's x-coordinate is getting larger by 1, and the line's y-coordinate is decreasing by 1 each time. (-1, 4) and (0, 3) will be the next two coordinates for the line.

40. D: If lines A and B are parallel, then the two indicated angles are alternate interior angles, making them congruent. Thus, if A and B are parallel, then θ = 80°.

41. A: The Sine of <A is the ratio of the length of the opposite side of the triangle to the length of the hypotenuse, or $\text{Sin } 60 = \frac{BC}{AC}$. To calculate the value of BC, isolate that value in the expression. If one multiplies both sides of the equation by the length of the hypotenuse, AC, one is left with the equation AC(Sin 60)=BC.

42. D: Students in 8th grade should be able to use basic algebraic concepts to analyze both proportional and non-proportional linear relationships. Remember that in a proportional relationship between x and y, the ratio between the two variables is constant. In a non-proportional relationship, the ratio is varied; in other words, the graph of the ratio between x and y will not be a straight line. Algebraic concepts are introduced in previous grades, but this standard is not expected to be used consistently until 8th grade.

43. D: The area of the garden is based upon the formula 1/2bh, in which b equals the base of the triangle and h equals the height of the triangle. However, only the length of the base is known. Because the problem includes a right triangle, the Pythagorean Theorem $(a^2 + b^2 = c^2)$ can be used to derive the unknown length. The hypotenuse, C, is given as . $\sqrt{369}$ The value of A is 12. Therefore, $12^2 + b^2 = (\sqrt{369})^2$ and b=15. By multiplying ½(12)(15), we find the correct answer, or 90 square feet.

44. A: The first step is to calculate the area left to paint. The total length is 15ft., so 2/5 the total length (the portion already painted) is 6ft. Then, multiply 6 ft. and 7.5 ft. (height of the wall). There are 56.25 ft^2 left to paint. The painter will need more than two gallons to paint the rest of the wall, since two gallons would cover 50 ft^2. Three gallons of paint costs $18.75 ($6.25/gallon x 3). Therefore, choice A lists the least amount the painter can spend.

- 39 -

45. B: There is a common misconception that English-language learners find it easier to learn math because this subject does not depend on a foreign language as much as it does on numbers. However, this assumption is based on the belief that all English-language learners use a common set of numbers, which is untrue for students that hail from various parts of the globe. Also, it is untrue that language does not play a major role in math instruction; in fact, it can be harder for some students to learn math because they are attempting to understand numeric principles without the benefit of a common language for explanation. Choice A, C and D are all beneficial techniques for instruction of English-language learners.

46. B: The gradient of a straight line refers to the slope of the line. This concept is vital to understanding linear equations. Choices A and C may be introduced during similar studies. However, *all* linear equations will involve gradients. Choice D suggests that quadrilaterals may be related to linear equations; however, the two concepts are not directly related.

47. B: The first step in solving for the standard deviation is to find the mean of all the values. In this case, the mean is the average of all five recorded times. To calculate variance, calculate the average of the squared difference between the mean and each individual value. To find the standard deviation, take the square root of the variance. Choice B displays the appropriate formula, while all other choices contain gaps in the formula.

48. C: The quartile is found by separating any set of data into four equal parts. The most common way to determine quartile is to divide the total set in two, and then repeat that process with each half of the data. In this data, the set of 60 can be divided by four, creating divisions every 15 digits. The four quartiles are: 1-15, 16-30, 31-45, and 46-60. Because 37 falls within the third group, Matt was in the 3rd quartile.

49. A: $2^3 \times 3^2$
Explanation: $72 = 8 \times 9 = 2 \times 4 \times 3 \times 3 = 2 \times 2 \times 2 \times 3 \times 3 = 2^3 \times 3^2$
8 times 9 equal 72. 2 times 2 times 2 equal 8. 3 times 3 equal 9. 2 and 3 are both prime numbers. 2 times 2 times 2 equal 2^3. 3 times 3 equal 3^2. 2^3 times 3^2 equals 72.

50. D: $x = 6$, $y = 11$ Explanation: When $x = 4$, $y = 3(4) - 1$; $12 - 1 = 11$; $y = 11$. When $y = 17$, $17 = 3x - 1$; $18 = 3x$; $x = 6$.

51. C: Students often struggle with money, even though it is a familiar and real-world concept, because there are multiple aspects to consider. In order to do these problems accurately, students must be able to add and subtract decimals. However, they must also understand the practical applications of this concept in their lives. Choices A and B both use test material that will improve this skill without addressing the concept itself. Students need to understand how to make change in the "real world," as well as how to complete a word problem on a test. Choice C addresses the money on a conceptual level in a fun way, combined with monitoring test practice to make sure the students are translating this knowledge to this context. Choice D only addresses one aspect of this issue, without connecting the interrelated skills in a meaningful way.

52. C: Formative assessment refers to any kind of evaluation by a teacher that helps guide her instruction. In mathematics instruction, teachers need to know exactly what the students have mastered in order to teach them appropriately because so many principles must be taught consecutively and in appropriate order. Conversations, class work and homework are all examples

of formative assessments. These practices help teachers know where students might need more help and where instruction should be focused.

53. C: Find the sum of 0.1, 0.3, 0.2 and 0.15. Multiply this sum by $2,200. Subtract this product from $2,200. Multiply the difference by 4.
Explanation: 0.1 + 0.3 + 0.2 + 0.15 = 0.75; $2,200 x 0.75 = $1,650; $2,200 - $1,650 = $550; $550 x 4 = $2,200.
Add 0.1, 0.3, 0.2, and 0.15 to find that Donna spends 0.75 of each month's income. Multiply 0.75 by $2,200 to find that she spends $1,650 each month. Subtract $1,650 from $2,200 to determine that she saves $550 per month. ⅓ of a year is 4 months. Multiply $550 by 4 to find that she could save $2,200 in one-third of a year.

54. C: $94.50 Explanation: ($8.50 x 4) + ($6.50 x 2) + $8.50 + ($5.50 x 3) + ($7.50 x 3) = $34 + $13 + $8.50 + $16.50 + $22.50 = $94.50
Multiply $8.50 by 4 to find the amount paid by adult members ($34). Multiply $6.50 by 2 to find the amount paid by senior citizen members ($13). One senior citizen who is not is member costs $8.50. Multiply $5.50 by 3 to find the amount paid for children who are members ($16.50). Multiply $7.50 by 3 to find the amount paid for children who are not members ($22.50). Add $34, $13, $8.50, $16.50, and $22.50 to find the total amount paid for admission ($94.50).

55. D: 17.5 miles Explanation: 58mph x 3 ½ hours= 203 miles; 63 mph x 3 ½ hours = 220.5 miles; 220.5 – 203 = 17.5 miles
Multiply 58 mph by 3 ½ hours to find that Ashley traveled 203 miles. Multiply 63 mph by 3 ½ hours to find that Catherine traveled 220.5 miles. Subtract 203 from 220.5 to determine that they were 17.5 miles apart.

56. A: 10 inches Explanation: Multiply the length of the rectangle by 2, subtract the product from the rectangle's perimeter, and divide by 2 to find the width of the rectangle (25 inches x 2 = 50 inches; 58 inches – 50 inches = 8 inches; 8 inches ÷ 2 = 4 inches). Multiply 25 inches by 4 inches to find the rectangle's area (25 inches x 4 inches = 100 square inches). Find the square root of 100 to determine the length of one side of the square (10 inches).

57. A: Explanation: 1/3 of 75 = 25; 75-25 = 50; 50: 10 = 5:1
Multiply 1/3 times 75 to find 25. Subtract 25 stickers from the original 75 smiley-face stickers so that now Mrs. Tucker at 50 smiley-face stickers. There is now a 50 to 10 ratio of smiley-face to star stickers. 50 to 10 can be simplified to 5 to 1.

58. B: The student enjoys reading. Explanation: There is no data to suggest or infer that the student enjoys reading.

59. C: To find the probability of an event, divide the number of favorable outcomes by the total number of outcomes. When there are two events in which the first depends on the second, multiply the first ratio by the second ratio. In the first part of the problem, the probability of choosing a licorice jelly bean is two out of twenty possible outcomes, or $\frac{2}{20}$. Then, because one jelly bean has already been chosen, there are four cinnamon beans out of a total of 19, or $\frac{4}{19}$. By multiplying the two ratios and dividing by a common denominator, one arrives at the final probability of $\frac{2}{95}$.

60. C: If the rate of violent crimes per month is anything like it is the year before, it will be greatest in the summer months, as there is a spike in the data on the graph during the summer months. While there is some fluctuation up and down throughout the entire year, these months are well beyond the numbers of the other months and represent the only upward trend in the graph.

History/Social Studies

61. C: As Europeans arrived, they brought many changes along with them. Guns and horses became much more prevalent in a short period of time. New diseases struck many Native Americans who had no immunity to the foreign illnesses. Europeans also brought with them many Christian missionaries who established missions and churches in the area. There were, however, a vast number of Native Americans living in separate groups of various sizes. Some groups and tribes joined forces to fight the Europeans, but others continued to fight amongst themselves, a continuation of struggles originating before the newcomers arrived.

62. A: Mary is describing the effects of the War of 1812 through this graphic organizer, which she has done accurately in this graph. However, the boxes on the bottom are somewhat vague, describing independence from Britain and industrial growth. By re-organizing her graph, Mary will demonstrate that the Industrial Revolution grew out of the War of 1812. Because industrial production grew, a new railroad system was built, production and refining was increased, and America relied less on foreign imports. All of these boxes are effects, or supporting details, of the War of 1812 and the Industrial Revolution.

63. D: Manifest Destiny refers to the belief that United States settlers could and had the right to expand into the western part of the country. This concept sometimes is believed to suggest that Americans had the divine or destined right to occupy all of North America. The term Manifest Destiny is commonly used as the historical term for the basis of expansion into the western territories in the late 1700's and early 1800's.

64. A: The American Civil Rights movement arose to address the disproportionate lack of power of African Americans in the United States. Civil leaders of all backgrounds joined to fight for monetary, professional, cultural and voting rights for African Americans during the 1960's. The oppression inherent in the years leading up to the Civil Rights movement is much like the racial segregation in South Africa before 1994, called *apartheid*. Under this system, white citizens possessed far more power and wealth than their Black counterparts, who experienced similar disenfranchisement. By studying *apartheid*, students can gain a better understanding of important historical events and their effect on culture, as well as relationships between cultures across the globe.

65. C: To achieve Roosevelt's goals, a great deal of money had to be spent, and the national debt skyrocketed. Millions of poor families received welfare, many jobs were created, and labor unions were strengthened with passage of the National Labor Relations Act.

66. C: Ms. Fisher wants to support what the students are reading in English class, thereby integrating their studies. The integration of disciplines deepens students' understanding of the relationship between culture, history, science, and the individual. By studying parts of Japanese culture and the social ramifications of World War II, students will enjoy a richer experience while reading about one woman's true story. Their knowledge of history and social sciences will help them understand the main character fully and make educated judgments about the story.

67. A: Brown v. Board of Education was decided in 1954. Rosa Parks was arrested in 1955. The lunch counter sit-ins were staged in 1960. The March on Washington took place in 1963.

68. C: In the social sciences, the term "prehistory" refers to the period before history was recorded in writing. Because various civilizations developed writing at different times, periods considered prehistoric vary from culture to culture.

69. C: Pope Urban II's plan for an army made up of previously trained military personnel was thwarted by the popular excitement concerning the First Crusade. This led to the creation of large armies primarily made up of untrained, unskilled, undisciplined, and ill- or unequipped soldiers, most of whom were recruited from the poorest levels of society. These armies were the first to set forth on the Crusade, which became known as the People's Crusade. Even though some of these armies contained knights, they were ultimately ineffective as fighting forces. These armies were prone to rioting and raiding surrounding areas for food and supplies and were viewed as a destabilizing influence by local leaders. They were defeated in battle and many converted to Islam to avoid being killed.

70. A: Genghis Khan, also spelled Chinggis Khan, was the son of a minor Mongol chieftain, born circa 1162 AD. His birth name was Temujin and he grew up in poverty, but gradually built his own power base to include a confederacy of Mongol clans. He was named Genghis Khan, or universal ruler, in 1206.
Attila the Hun was the 5th Century Hunnic leader who led his people to attack into Western Europe, going as far as Gaul (modern day France).
The leader of China's 19th Century Taiping Rebellion was Hong Xiuquan, also known as Hong Houxiu.

71. D: The Ka'ba is an ancient structure Muslims consider holy; it was purportedly built by Abraham. The Ka'ba's location in Mecca is the central reason for Mecca's importance to Muslims. Although Muhammad was born in Mecca, that fact is not the primary reason for Mecca's importance in Islam; the location of the Ka'ba is more important. This eliminates option A. Option C can be rejected because Muhammad fled from Mecca to Medina in 622 A.D., not the other way around. Option B can be rejected because Muslims believe the Second Coming will occur in Damascus, not Mecca.

72. C: Exploration between the 15th and 17th centuries resulted in contact between European cultures and many previously unknown or little-known cultures. Navigation techniques improved, food and other goods were imported, and the New World began to be settled. Rather than declining in influence, England became a more prominent imperial power during this era.

73. D: Gutenberg's press used moveable metal type which he formed casting a metal alloy into molds made for each character. These individual pieces were then organized by letter. The letters were loaded into composing sticks that were then loaded into a metal form to create printing plates. As the printing press spread across Europe, printers began using woodcut prints to include illustrations in their products.
While Gutenberg is generally given credit for the invention of moveable type, in the 1040s Pi Sheng, a Chinese inventor and alchemist, created moveable type using clay characters which were then pressed into wax-coated plates for printing.

74. A: With the proliferation of the World Wide Web, people of all ages and backgrounds have access to a vast repository of information. With this information, students can pursue interests and

ideas from any place with an internet connection. Many internet websites have come about that are solely dedicated to assisting children in finding information. However, the internet also contains much information that is false or misleading, because there is very little oversight of its content. Therefore, teachers must educate students on how to determine what information they find online is reliable and can be trusted as accurate.

75. C: Teachers should make every effort to illustrate for students that all Social Studies and other academic skills function together for deeper understanding.

76. B: Being a citizen involves multiple responsibilities and exercising just as many freedoms with responsibility. Citizenship rests on the assumption that the individual will behave according to social rules and in a way that is best for the society as a whole. The best way to teach young students to be citizens is to allow them to actually *be* citizens. This scenario suggests that all students have jobs that contribute to their classroom in some way: sharpening pencils, watering plants, gathering papers, and various other tasks. The students also get practice identifying important issues and voting democratically upon them to come to a decision. While they may not vote on every single issue that arises, the teacher can guide students to participate in effective ways. With this practice, students will become accustomed to helping others and contributing to their community in a positive way.

77. C: Judicial review refers to a court's ability to determine if laws or trial decisions made by lower courts are constitutional or legal. This concept arises in instruction regarding the branches of government. The executive, judicial, and legislative branches are often discussed at their simplest levels, giving each branch a general purpose. However, when discussing checks and balances in government, students must understand how and why government is limited in order to maintain democracy and individual freedoms.

78. A: In *Dred Scott v Sandford*, the slave Dred Scott attempted to gain his freedom based upon the fact that he had lived with his owners in abolitionist states during his lifetime. The Supreme Court denied his claim, stating that he was not a citizen of the United States and therefore could not bring suit in a federal court. This case illustrates the fact that this nation has been debating the concept of citizenship, and who can become a citizen, for centuries. Students will find their understanding of current events deepened by historical knowledge of laws and social belief systems.

79. B: Lines of longitude, which run north-south from pole to pole, are used to separate time zones. Houston, Texas, and Fargo, North Dakota, which are on almost the exact same line of longitude, are both in the Central Time Zone; however, they are not in the same state, do not have the same climate, and are not equidistant from the equator. To calculate distance from the equator, the latitude of the city would need to be known.

80. C: The area depicted by the map includes many countries considered to make up the Middle Eastern part of the world, which lies between Europe and Asia. Choice A is true for some major world religions, such as Islam, Christianity, and Judaism, yet there are other religions that have originated in other parts of the world, such as Buddhism and African traditional religions.

81. A: The Middle East region relies heavily on its export businesses, a large component of which is oil production. By adding information regarding commerce and industry, students can draw conclusions about similarities and connections between the two different places. While there are many facets to study of an entire global region, the primary similarity, or common interest, between

their state and Middle Eastern states is in industry. Political and religious divisions are not common between the two entities, aside from the fact that they exist.

82. B: The North American Free Trade Agreement was established in 1994 by the United States, Canada, and Mexico in an effort to minimize trade barriers among the continent's three nations.

83. C: Physical geography focuses on processes and patterns in the natural environment. What people eat in any given geographic region is largely dependent on such environmental factors as climate and the availability of arable land. Religion, family, and language may all be affected by geographical factors, but they are not as immediately affected as dietary preferences.

84. C: Part of middle school economics study, includes the various kinds of industries. There are three generally accepted forms of industry in all economies: primary, secondary, and tertiary. Primary industry includes the harvesting of raw materials, including farming, mining, etc. Secondary industries process these materials. Tertiary businesses offer services to individuals, such as healthcare offices, drycleaners, restaurants, and so on. The dentist offers a service to patients or clients, thus making it a tertiary industry.

85. C: The terms *recession* and *depression* appeared in curricula more frequently as the national and international economies dipped in 2008 and 2009. All students are expected to understand how the United States' free enterprise system operates, as well as how other societies function economically. Identifying and defining periods of economic recession comprise a very relevant lesson in this discipline. There is no universal definition of an economic depression, although some economists suggest that this phenomenon yields a decline in GDP that exceeds 10% or lasts for several years.

86. B: A strict constructionist, Jefferson argued that that the Constitution did not make any provision for the creation of a federal bank. Jefferson was a leader of the Democratic-Republicans who opposed the establishment of a powerful central government. He believed that the Bank would give an unfair advantage to the more industrial northern states.

87. B: Lower interest rates allow banks to lend out more money, which serves to stimulate consumer spending. Increased spending tends to raise, not lower, prices. The Federal Reserve Board is not actively involved in international trade. The fear of inflation usually leads to a raise in interest rates.

88. C: The Social Sciences are many, and include multiple disciplines that are interconnected. Anthropology is the study of human beings and culture, and therefore this choice best falls into the category of Social Sciences. Choices A, C and D constitute scientific careers, but do not have obvious social links. Choice A focuses on biological studies, which involve humans but usually do not address social behaviors and trends. Choice B refers to the study of insects and choice C to the study of Physics. Neither choice addresses social developments of humans.

89. D: Louisiana's population increased between 1990 and 2000, but in 2005 Hurricane Katrina struck the coast of Louisiana. As a result of this hurricane, many residents lost their homes, jobs, and even their lives. The mass exodus of Louisiana residents to neighboring states to find homes and work in the aftermath of the hurricane resulted in a significant, though temporary, drop in the state's population.

90. B: Students are more motivated to inquire and learn new things when the topic at hand is relevant to their real lives. Since Amorosa is obviously looking forward to her *Quinceañera,* she may enjoy researching similar celebrations and customs inherent in other cultures. By relating this cultural research to an event she is anticipating, her teacher will help her identify relevant similarities across many cultures. Amorosa will also have an opportunity to practice understanding contrasts between various events as well as cultures throughout the project that will aid her in deepening cultural awareness in the future.

Science

91. A: The nucleolus is located in the nucleus of the cell, and is responsible for the transcription and assembly of r-RNA. Roughly spherical in shape, this organelle is not surrounded by any type of membrane. Chromoplasts b., mitochondria c., and endoplasmic reticulum d. can all be classified as membrane bound organelles. They are responsible for storing and synthesizing pigments, energy production, and the transportation of proteins, respectively.

92. C: The top portion of the illustration shows the molecular structure of glucose, which is used by the body for energy in completing tasks like walking, talking or writing. Sucrose, in the bottom picture, is made up of one glucose molecule and one fructose molecule. Fructose is a foreign sugar that is converted to fat by the body and not used for any benefit. Therefore, glucose is the sugar used for energy in the body; sucrose does contain glucose, but also contains fructose which converts to fat.

93. B: Genetics encompasses the concept of traits and how certain traits are passed from parents to offspring. The traits listed in the left-hand column are commonly studied in the field of genetics, as they are passed down based upon combinations of recessive and dominant genes. Choices A and C are not directly related to the chart. Choice D refers to the process by which organisms adapt to the environment. However, the traits listed in this chart are not vital to the survival of a species, making choice B a better fit.

94. C: Animal dissection is a controversial topic among science educators of young students. Some individuals feel that the practice is harmful to all involved. However, the historical basis for dissection aligns most closely with choice C, in that it is said to help students experience anatomy and scientific concepts in a tangible way. Regardless of a teacher's personal standpoint on animal dissection or use in the classroom, he must be educated in the historical foundations of scientific practices and be prepared to help students work through controversial issues.

95. C: The leaves on a tree appear to be green because that is the color of the light that is being reflected. All other colors are absorbed a. , and are not perceived by the human eye. Refraction b. is when light bends slightly, usually when it enters one medium from another. Diffraction d. is when light bends around obstacles or spreads out after it passes through a small opening.

96. B: Biodiversity deals with living organisms and their interconnections within an environment. We know that the local pond is the best environment in which to observe a contained ecosystem. Gas-powered boats leave harmful chemicals in the pond water, which will be absorbed into the ground and by animals living in and around the water. Those animals will be contaminated with those chemicals, as will plants growing from the groundwater. By eliminating these chemical contaminants, the protected pond environment will host healthy and thriving species for many years to come.

97. B: Biodiversity refers to the wide diversity of living things on our planet, all of which are interconnected and affect one another. These living organisms can be studied within a particular biome, ecosystem, or the Earth as a whole. If students plan to visit a site and keep field journals, then they will need to observe a diverse group of organisms in their natural environment. The local pond contains a complete individual ecosystem, including water cycles, rock cycles, animals and life cycles. The zoo, in choice A, contains diverse animal life, but these animals are not living in their natural environment. Choices C and D would be informative field trips, but do not provide the life systems relevant to the topic of biodiversity.

98. A: According to natural selection, organisms with traits that are well suited to their environments are the ones that survive. In this instance, gray moths were able to blend in with soot-covered trees better than white moths. Therefore, the gray moths survived and reproduced. Genetic drift b. refers to the random changes in gene frequencies over time. Sexual selection c. refers to the fact that organisms compete for or choose mates. Punctuated equilibrium d. states that evolution occurs quickly after long periods of little change.

99. C: Rhinoceros horns and human hair are both made of compressed fibers of keratin. They are homologous characteristics, meaning they are inherited from a common ancestor, even though they may serve various functions in different species. Ancestral characteristics a. are unmodified characteristics found in common ancestors, not the species that developed from them. Detrimental characteristics b. are those that interfere with normal functioning or threaten an organism's survival. Analogous characteristics d. are not evolutionarily related, but serve similar functions in different species.

100. D: Population size is not relevant when determining an organism's evolutionary history. Population sizes vary over time according to many factors, so no real conclusions can be drawn from this information. Fossil record placement a. can help determine when species developed and how they are related to other organisms. Studying an organism's anatomy b. is useful because ancestors can be identified by looking at physical characteristics like bone structure and appendages. Studying distribution among continents d. can help determine where an organism originated.

101. C: The sun is mainly composed of hydrogen and helium. During nuclear fusion reactions, hydrogen is transformed into helium and energy that is released in the form of visible light. This reaction produces 85% of the sun's energy. Hydrogen is transformed into helium, not the other way around a. Lithium produces helium only, and is not the primary process that creates sunlight b. Helium does form beryllium and a gamma ray, but is not how most of the sun's light is produced.

102. B: As the earth travels around the sun, it tilts towards the sun or away from it, depending on where it is in its orbit. This tilt is what determines the seasons. The earth is tilted towards the sun in summer and away from it in winter. Elevation a. and latitude c. of an area remain constant throughout the year, so they cannot account for the changing of the seasons. Air masses d. can influence the weather, but don't determine the seasons.

103. C: In order to change the structure and form of rocks, intense or sustained changes must occur. Plate tectonics cause intense heat and pressure to modify rock structures. The water cycle can effect cooling and erosion that will also affect this cycle. Volcanic eruptions lead to melting and re-forming in a more effective way than would global warming, which is a much more gradual process.

104. A: During volcanic eruptions, magma is expelled. As a result, the emptied area is not able to support the rock above it. It collapses, creating a crater-like formation known as a caldera. Calderas are created when rocks move down, not up b. A caldera is not a class of volcano c.; it is a volcanic feature that occasionally forms after eruptions. It is not the cooling of lava d. that accounts for calderas, but rather the expulsion of magma.

105. A: A shortage of habitable land was never a factor that stopped the human population from increasing. Even today, North America has only about 32 people per square mile, so land availability has never been a huge problem. Advances in agriculture b. allowed more food to be produced on the same amount of land. Better food availability was a factor in population growth, as was improved sanitation c. , which resulted in less sickness and disease. Understanding the causes of communicable diseases d. resulted in fewer deaths.

106. C: The theory of anchored instruction involves a problem-based learning model. Students receive background knowledge through stories or other forms of learning and then use this information to complete various modules or activities. Within an anchored instruction-based lesson, all information necessary to solve problems or answer questions must be included in the format. In this way, students are learning something new by working independently within a procedural scaffold. In choice C, students read necessary background information and then use this, along with a scale-model, to answer questions about the solar system.

107. D: Most of the evaporation in the atmosphere comes from the earth's oceans. When water from the oceans evaporates, the temperature in those large bodies of water is reduced. When the oceans are cooler on their surfaces, the planet's temperatures are cooler. Without the cooling that evaporation affords, the earth itself would grow warmer and warmer, contributing to the greenhouse effect and global warming phenomena.

108. C: Organisms that thrive in environments where other living things could not survive – such as around hot thermal vents found under the sea – are often known as extremophiles. These organisms are typically microorganisms like bacteria, which are prokaryotes. Protists a., are classified as eukaryotes b., which are not typically found in extreme environments. Metazoans d. are multi-cellular, eukaryotic organisms. Like all eukaryotes, metazoans do not thrive near thermal vents or in other extreme environments.

109. A: The vast majority of the earth (approximately 70%) b. is covered in water. Therefore, approximately 30% of the earth is solid land. Of all the water on earth, only about 2% of that is fresh water, and most of that is present in glaciers and the polar ice caps. Therefore 98% (100% - 2%) of the earth's water is the salt water (saline) found in the oceans.

110. B: The water at the surface of the ocean will usually be slightly warmer than the air. It evaporates, enters the air, and then rises, making the atmosphere slightly warmer. Radiation a. is the active emitting of energy from an object. Thermoregulation c. is the ability of an organism to control its body temperature. Transduction d. is the transfer of DNA among different bacteria by viruses.

111. A: Pure water will always freeze at the same temperature: 0° Celsius, or 32° Fahrenheit. The temperature at which iron ore will melt b. varies depending on the types of impurities that are present in the substance. The human population size c. has been changing ever since humans first inhabited the earth. The time the sun rises, d. varies according to the time of year and the location of the observer.

112. B: A physical change refers to one in which the substance being acted upon maintains its chemical composition. Thus, any change in which a substance melts, freezes, or evaporates is a physical change, as is one in which the substance simply changes its shape. A chemical change is one in which the substance changes in chemical substance. The only choice in which a new chemical entity is formed is that in which rust forms on a nail.

113. B: Benzene, an organic compound, is classified as a carcinogen by the U.S. Department of Health and Human Services. The chemical has been linked to kidney cancer, leukemia, and other health problems. For that reason, benzene is not allowed in school laboratories. Lead a. can harm individuals, particularly children, if ingested, but is not considered a carcinogen. Aspartame c. is an artificial sweetener found in many foods and beverages. Methanol d., or methyl alcohol, can be fatal if ingested, but is not considered a potential carcinogen.

114. B: This is related to Newtown's second law of motion, expressed as F = m*a. To determine whether the statement is true, let the value of "a" be 2. Let the mass of the first block be 1 (F = 2). The mass of the second block is 2. Therefore, F = 2*2; F = 4. It would take twice as much force, not three times as much. a. and c. are examples of the law of inertia. d. is an example of Newton's third law.

115. D: By measuring the mass of the wood before and after burning and then calculating the difference between the two masses, the amount of matter lost during burning can be determined. Since different types of gases with different molecular weights are released, calculating the total number of molecules would not allow the mass to be calculated a. The gases emitted combine with oxygen in the air, making b. an unsuitable approach. The weight of the ash alone c. wouldn't be helpful without knowing the original mass.

116. B: All of the items in the box are objects designed to be put in motion. Bikes and skateboards need energy created by the rider's motions in order to move, while the other vehicles require fuel or electricity in order to move as they should. Discussing the ways in which these real-life items can be put into motion deepens students' relevant knowledge about energy sources and movement. Choices A and D are possible activities that could be used in class. However, these discussions are a bit less relevant to direct instruction than the correct answer choice, B.

117. D: The conductivity of a material *decreases* with increased vibrational motion of the atoms. The exception is semiconductive materials. Superconductive materials have increased conductivity when the vibrational motion of the atoms decreases. LASERS, MASERS, and photoelectric sensors are all applications of quantum physics that are related to atomic emissions, not changes in the vibrational motion of atoms.

118. C: Wavelength determines the nature of the electromagnetic wave (i.e. radio waves, microwaves, infrared radiation, visible light, ultraviolet radiation, X-rays, gamma rays, etc.).
Sound pitch depends on the frequency (a) of the sound wave.
The loudness of a sound depends on the amplitude (b) of the sound wave.
The speed of light (d) is a constant.
The period of a wave (e) is defined as 1 divided by the frequency of the wave.

119. A: Sound pitch depends on the frequency of the sound wave.
The loudness of a sound depends on the amplitude of the sound wave (b).

Wavelength (c) determines the nature of the electromagnetic wave (i.e. radio waves, microwaves, infrared radiation, visible light, ultraviolet radiation, X-rays, gamma rays, etc.).
The speed of sound (d) is a constant for any specific medium. For example, the speed of sound in air is 340 m/s.
The period of a wave (e) is defined as 1 divided by the frequency of the wave.

120. A: Alpha particles are essentially helium nuclei with a mass of 4 amu. Beta rays (b) are electrons released when a neutron decomposes to form a proton and an electron. The mass of an electron (beta) is approximately 1/2000th amu. Gamma rays (c) are high energy, short wavelength, high frequency electromagnetic waves. Gamma rays have no mass. X-rays (d) and ultraviolet light (e) are also electromagnetic waves and have no mass.

Practice Test #2

Practice Questions

Literature and Language Studies

1. At the beginning of the school year, Ms. Walker conducted a words correct per minute (WCPM) test for Amelia, a student in her 7th grade reading class. Amelia averaged 200 words per minute on two unpracticed readings at her grade level. Which of the following should Ms. Walker infer from Amelia's performance?
    a. Amelia's reading comprehension is well above average
    b. Amelia's reading fluency is well above average
    c. Amelia's reading comprehension is somewhat below average
    d. Amelia's reading fluency is somewhat below average

2. Mr. Heath has noticed that some of the students in his 8th grade reading class quickly become distracted and frustrated during silent reading sessions, and he suspects that the cause is poor reading fluency. Which of the following activities could help him evaluate this suspicion?
    a. Asking the students to read unfamiliar grade-level texts aloud and noting whether they read with proper speed, accuracy, and intonation
    b. Giving the students a vocabulary test
    c. Finding out if English is the students' native language
    d. Asking the students directly why they get frustrated when they read

3. Which of the following is an example of metacognition?
    a. Pausing periodically during reading to assess your comprehension of the text
    b. Retelling a story after reading it
    c. Identifying components of text structure in a narrative text
    d. Being able to read without pausing to decode words

4. Which of the following is an example of a strategy that would help develop students' intrinsic motivation to read?
    a. Providing books that resonate with students' interests and personal experiences
    b. Having students read for a set period of time every night and requiring parents to sign a reading log for the student
    c. Collaborating with teachers from other subject areas to assign readings that that are relevant to what students are learning across the curriculum
    d. Conducting intensive decoding and vocabulary practice

5. The parents of a gifted student in Ms. Sanchez' 6th grade reading class have asked for help in selecting appropriate summer reading material for their son. Which of the following would be the most appropriate way for Ms. Sanchez to respond to this request?
    a. Tell them to ask the other parents what their students are reading
    b. Suggest that they use an Internet search engine to find relevant books
    c. Provide them with a list of books that are at the student's reading level
    d. Offer to forward their request to the school librarian

6. Which of the following statements is true of both print and visual media?
    a. Print media can be used to address serious journalistic subjects, but film can only be used to entertain viewers
    b. Unlike narratives in print form, film narratives typically lack the traditional elements of plot, such as exposition and climax
    c. It is generally agreed that films are more effective at persuading individuals to change their views than written texts
    d. While film producers can influence the viewer's mood using music and lighting, writers must rely solely on literary conventions to invoke emotion.

7. Brian is in 5th grade and says he hates to read. He has performed poorly on a consistent basis on classroom work and standardized testing, specifically with regard to reading comprehension. He has complained of disliking the texts he is given to read in class, saying that they are too easy, too hard, or simply boring. What might be a first step that a teacher should take in working to improve Brian's comprehension skills?
    a. Deliver a reading comprehension assessment verbally, reading passages aloud to Brian and asking questions aloud. Analyze and monitor responses for comprehension.
    b. Ask Brian to select something he likes to read from outside class and allow him to read it aloud, after which he answers selected oral comprehension questions.
    c. Encourage Brian to read extensively, based on the belief that more practice yields better skill, which in turn builds motivation.
    d. Establish a rewards system with Brian. Agree upon a point value for each completed comprehension lesson or class work. As Brian accumulates points, establish a larger reward that he can earn based on the points he gains.

8. Which of the following would be considered a *critical* or *inferential* comprehension skill?
    a. Distinguishing between cause and effect
    b. Understanding word meanings
    c. Identifying literary techniques
    d. Recalling events in a story

9. Which of the following is the best way to utilize the various levels of reading comprehension within a classroom to help *all* students build comprehension skills?
    a. Use worksheets of varying difficulty to assign as class work.
    b. Allow students who are stronger in reading comprehension to teach small lessons throughout the week.
    c. Form groups that include students of varying abilities, and assign each person to lead discussion on an appropriate topic or question based upon ability level.
    d. Assign partners or buddies, using a student who is stronger in comprehension to help one who is weaker complete class work.

10. Mr. Hawking is planning to show his students that it is possible to communicate ideas without actually speaking. How can he utilize the novel his students are reading in class to teach these concepts?

a. Have the students form groups and collaborate to adapt the novel into a play, which they can then act out for the class.

b. Play a game in which students draw simple pictures of characters, ideas, or events in the novel. The team that can correctly guess the largest number of 'pictograms' wins.

c. As a class, agree upon common bodily actions or hand gestures that represent certain aspects of everyday life. Practice using them each day to communicate without speaking.

d. Ask students to draw pictures and isolate new or interesting words to record in their journals and share with the class during "share time."

11. The following excerpt is an example of what kind of assessment?

Date:
Name:
It took me __ minutes to read the first 10 pages of *The Trial of Dabney Moore.*
1. Describe the main character's personality in this book.
2. Why do you think Dabney chose to confess his crimes to the police?
3. If you were in Dabney's position, would you have acted in the same way? Why or why not?

a. Student response form
b. Cloze-style assessment
c. Fluency and articulation evaluation
d. Informal reading inventory

12. Which of the following statements most accurately describes the role of 4th through 8th grade teachers with respect to fostering students' oral language development?

a. Because most students in grades 4 through 8 have already mastered oral language, teachers in these grades may safely concentrate on other aspects of language development

b. Teachers in grades 4 through 8 should monitor students for evidence of language delays, but activities designed to enhance oral language skills are not necessary

c. Teachers with students in grades 4 through 8 should spend more class time on developing students' oral language skills than on developing reading and writing skills because oral language skills are more critical to academic success

d. Most students in grades 4 through 8 have mastered basic oral language skills, but teachers should still incorporate class activities designed to enhance higher-order oral language skills

13. A student who grasps the alphabetic principle understands that...

a. There is a systematic relationship between sounds and letters
b. The letters of the alphabet are arranged in a specific alphabetical order
c. The letters that comprise words can be broken down into syllables
d. Letters can be blended to create sounds that are not in the alphabet

14. How should a teacher get information about her students' specific strengths and weaknesses?

a. Check her students' scores on state-mandated, criterion-referenced tests
b. Examine her students' scaled scores on norm-referenced verbal intelligence tests
c. Administer an informal reading inventory such as the BRI, QRI-4, CRI-CFC, or ARI
d. Find out what reading grades the students got last year

15. Mr. Hammond is teaching his middle school writing class a unit on Internet etiquette. Which of the following would likely be considered a breach of Internet etiquette?
   a. Writing an email in all capital letters
   b. Disagreeing with another participant on a discussion board
   c. Addressing the recipient of an email as "Sir or Madam" when the recipient's name and gender is not known
   d. Using multiple exclamation points in a comment about an online video to express enjoyment of the video

16. Mr. Wan has assigned his class an expository text about the benefits of recycling. Based on that text, which of the following is an example of a reading comprehension question (or questions) that assesses evaluative comprehension skills?
   a. What are the three main reasons that the author thinks people should recycle?
   b. Do you think that the author recycles? Why or why not?
   c. Where does the author say that people can find information about recycling programs in their communities?
   d. Do you agree with the author's argument that recycling is important? Why or why not?

17. Which of the following activities is an example of guided practice in reading comprehension?
   a. A teacher models the strategy of previewing
   b. A teacher provides differentiated texts for students at different reading levels
   c. A teacher asks students to perform a brief reading comprehension activity and then provides immediate feedback on the students' performance
   d. A teacher asks his or her class to read from the same text silently for 30 minutes and then leads a discussion about it

18. A student reading a text at his or her independent reading level...
   a. Should find the text fairly challenging and should frequently consult a dictionary or ask about the meaning of words
   b. Should find the text moderately challenging, but should recognize the vast majority (about 95 percent) of the words in the text
   c. Should find the text interesting enough that he or she becomes completely engrossed in it
   d. Should find the text easy to read without outside assistance of any kind

19. Graphic organizers can be used for which of the following purposes?
   a. To help students self-monitor as they read
   b. To assess reading comprehension
   c. To visually represent the text structure
   d. All of the above

20. Which of the following techniques represents the most effective overall approach for helping students succeed in reading tasks required for subjects like math, science, and social studies?
   a. Ensuring that students build an extensive vocabulary
   b. Consistently providing explicit instruction in expository text comprehension
   c. Teaching students to read visual data presentations such as graphs and charts
   d. Providing both fiction and nonfiction texts for students during silent reading

21. Which selection is most true regarding the use of journal writing in class?
   a. Student journals should always contain very structured assignments. Without specific instructions about what to write, the journals will not likely show improvement.
   b. Journals should never be graded to avoid the decrease of motivation. Students should always feel free to write whatever or however they feel at any given moment without fear of lower grades.
   c. Student journals provide space in which students can express their feelings and thoughts. Teachers should provide parameters on content, conventions, and expectations to ensure that students are utilizing what they have learned about the writing process.
   d. Parents and teachers can use journals as a resource to know more about the student. Teachers can use journal content to inform writing curriculum and instruction; parents can use their children's journals to gain insight about development.

22. Which of the following would *not* be used as instruction on writing conventions?
   a. Practice correcting sentences with incorrect punctuation.
   b. Re-writing work that is difficult to read due to word spacing and handwriting.
   c. Brainstorming details to support the main concepts in an essay.
   d. Checking spelling and using a dictionary and thesaurus to make sure that words are used correctly.

23. How can a teacher most effectively use assessment tools to communicate a student's progress to parents at conference time?
   a. Utilize standardized test scores to break down each category of literacy development and discuss skill levels.
   b. Show parents examples of the student's work across all aspects of his or her development and describe which areas are strongest and which areas need more work.
   c. Give the parents an overview of the student's progress along with one or two specific areas upon which to work at improving at home.
   d. Encourage students to be present in parent conferences to demonstrate reading skills and discuss plans for the coming term with both parents and teacher.

24. Which of the following is a classroom activity that would help develop students' understanding of the rules of pragmatics?
   a. Playing a game in which students must identify the parts of speech in sentences
   b. Reading a text and making inferences from it about what the author is like
   c. Conducting small group discussions followed by the students summarizing their discussion partners' comments on the discussion topic
   d. Using contextual clues and word analysis to infer the meanings of unfamiliar words

25. Students in a 7th-grade classroom arrive to see the following questions written on the board. Their teacher has graded the first writing assignment of the year. Which area of the writing process do you think she plans to address?

> -What am I most interested in about this topic?
> -How do I feel about this topic?
> -What do I want to say about this topic?
> -How can I say it so that my reader will understand what I mean?
> -What should I say first?
> -What details will prove my point?
> -What information is not important in this topic?

    a. Organization
    b. Idea development
    c. Persuasive writing
    d. Revision

26. Which choice is the most accurate and appropriate for quickly assessing students' reading fluency and comprehension skills at any given point?
    a. The teacher listens to each student read a short passage aloud and asks questions at the end to determine whether or not the student comprehends.
    b. Use a reading scheme or set that includes readers (short books), worksheets, comprehension activities, and applications at the end of each month.
    c. Assign worksheets that include both phonics work (to monitor fluency skills) and reading comprehension passages, followed by basic comprehension questions.
    d. Lead a group or class discussion on the major concepts in any given unit of study, allowing students to vocalize what they feel confident with and address areas where extra instruction may be needed.

27. Mrs. Nelson's 7th-grade students have been reading about the SQ3R (survey, question, read/write, review) method of studying. This study plan allows the student to survey, preview information, formulate questions based on that preview, and then read in order to answer those questions. The student will then make notes in relation to these questions as well as other information in the text. Reviewing questions and notes is the final step of this ongoing process. To what kind of reading assignment should the students practice applying their new study method?
    a. Poetry
    b. A social studies textbook
    c. Journal entries
    d. A fiction story

28. The 6th-grade students in Mrs. Nelson's class are currently reading an adventure story, which they are enjoying very much. However, there are multiple plotlines developing simultaneously and the story contains many characters. Which study/analytical skill can Mrs. Nelson introduce to support the students?
    a. Provide a "cheat sheet" containing synopses of each storyline and brief descriptions of the characters.
    b. Show the movie of the same story shown in class.
    c. Ask the students to pick characters and act out the story.
    d. Create a story map with the students in class that contains major events in each plotline and brief descriptions of the characters as they read the story.

29. A nationally-anticipated sporting event will be televised over the weekend, and Mr. Protos intends to incorporate this bit of the students' daily lives into his curriculum for teaching *viewing and representing*. This particular group of 8th-graders comprises Mr. Protos' Gifted and Talented English class and he would like to assign a bit of a challenge for them. Which assignment is the best blend of challenge and an already-existing event in the students' lives?

    a. Hold an informal discussion on Monday regarding the meaning of "televised sports and our social development." Allow the students to contribute ideas about how this event has been embedded into their social consciousness.

    b. Ask the students to journal about the sporting event as it happens, including predictions and reactions to its twists and turns. Discuss these real-time reactions in class on Monday.

    c. Ask the students to watch the commercials on "mute" and keep a log of what they think the ads are representing. Discuss the accuracy of the students' assumptions and interpretations on Monday.

    d. Assign a written report on the styles of athletes' dress, hair, and physical attributes and how these factors affect the viewing of—and engagement with—televised sports.

30. The Texas Essential Knowledge and Skills (TEKS) for grades 4 through 8 states that...

    a. Students are not expected to read grade-level texts fluently until 6th grade

    b. Students must meet specific words correct per minute (WCPM) metrics in each grade in order to demonstrate reading fluency

    c. Students in grades 4 through 8 are expected to read grade-level texts fluently

    d. English Language Learners (ELLs) are exempt from all reading fluency standards

Mathematics

31. Which of the following represent equivalent numbers?

    a. 50,000 and 5×10^3

    b. 0.400 and 4/100

    c. 3/4 and 0.75

    d. 10,000 and 10^5

32. A new dictionary costs $40. Thea bought the dictionary on sale for $30. Which best represents the discount obtained by Thea?

    a. 25%

    b. ½

    c. 10^2

    d. 10%

33. Find the value of $8 \times 4 + 6 \div 3 - 1$.

    a. 11 2/3

    b. 31

    c. 33

    d. 56

34. There are 26 classes in a school. 11 of them have 29 students each, and the rest have 25 students each. If there are 398 girls in the school, how many boys are there?

    a. 263

    b. 296

    c. 305

    d. 571

35. $4^2 + 15^3 \times (3^2)^3 - 5^4 \div 2^2 =$
    a. 423,718.75
    b. 617,853.5
    c. 2,459,733.75
    d. 2,460,234.75

36. Find the next two numbers in the following pattern:
      48, 12, 44, 11, 40, 10, 36, 9, ____, _____
    a. 35, 7
    b. 32, 8
    c. 28, 7
    d. 8, 32

Use the following graph to answer problems 37 and 38.

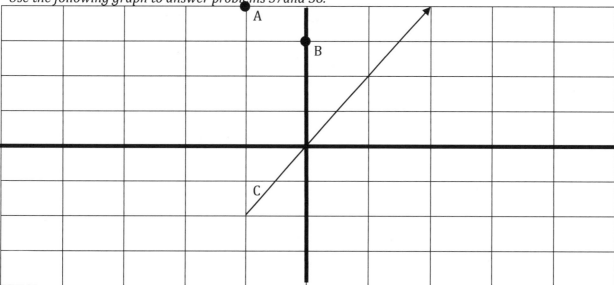

Assume that the gridlines indicate consecutive integers.

37. What is the equation of line C?
    a. y = 2/x
    b. y = -x
    c. y = 2x
    d. y = -x + 1

38. What would be the equation of a line drawn through points A and B?
    a. y = -x + 3
    b. y = x/x +4
    c. y = x/2 -3
    d. y = -x -5

39. Which line could be graphed from the equation y = 2x/x?

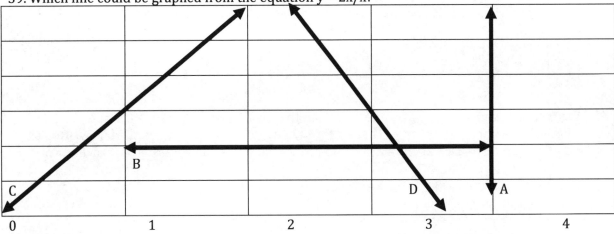

    a. Line A
    b. Line B
    c. Line C
    d. Line D

40. Find the slope of a line which passes through points (1, 3) and (7, 10).
    a. 3/10
    b. 5/3
    c. 7/6
    d. 13/8

41. Determine the limit of x^2 - 1/x - 1 as x approaches 1.
    a. -1
    b. 1
    c. -2
    d. 2

42. David is wrapping a box in which two faces are squares with sides of 4 inches, and four faces have a length 6 inches and a width of 4 inches. How many square inches of wrapping paper will he need to completely cover the box?
    a. 40
    b. 96
    c. 104
    d. 128

43. Use the information below to answer the question that follows.
        The Sun is 93 million miles away from the Earth.
Which of the following is the most accurate representation of this distance?
    a. 93^6
    b. 93×10^6
    c. 93×10^8
    d. 93×100^6

- 59 -

44. A rectangular wooden block is 48 in long, 30 in wide and 16 in high. If each cube of side 2 in is cut away from each of its corners, what is the volume of the wooden block left?
    a. 22,976 in³
    b. 23,008 in³
    c. 23,032 in³
    d. 23,040 in³

45. Which answer choice is a valid direct proof that the sum of two odd integers, x+y, is even?
    a. Because they are odd, x = 2a + 1 and y = 2b +1. The expression x + y can then be written as (2a + 1) + (2b + 1) = 2a + 2b + 2 = 2(a + b +1). Because this final expression clearly has a factor of two, x+y must be even.
    b. Assume y=13 and x=11. 13 + 24 = 24. 24 is even, therefore x + y is even.
    c. Let x + y = z, let z = 2c, let x = (2a + 1), and let y = (2b + 1). 2a + 1 + 2b + 1 = 2c → 2a + 2b = 2c - 2, therefore x + y is even.
    d. If x + y = z, where z is even, then x + y must be even.

46. The expression (2x+3)(x-2) can also be written as 2x ^ 2 – x – 6. Which of the following choices makes this transformation possible?
    a. The distributive property
    b. The commutative property
    c. The associative property
    d. The transformative property

47. Zac had $12y. He bought 3 cups of coffee at $ y/2 each and 2 bagels at $2y each. How much money did Zac have left?
    a. $4.25y
    b. $6.50y
    c. $8.50y
    d. $10.00y

48. Identify which rule describes the sequence -20, -15, -10, -5, . . .
    a. subtract +5
    b. add -5
    c. add +5
    d. multiply by -5

49. Natalie took 7 minutes to walk from her house to school. Her average speed was 80 feet/minute. How long would she take if her average speed was 70 feet/minute?
    a. 6 minutes
    b. 8 minutes
    c. 9 minutes
    d. 10 minutes

50. Which number line most accurately represents the inequality 4x ≤ 12?

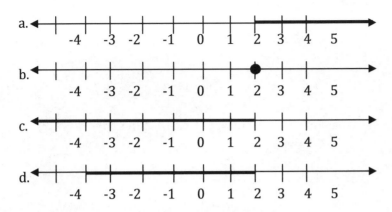

a.

b.

c.

d.

51. Patrick took 6 hours to travel from Greenville to Hightown at an average speed of 65 miles per hour. Saul took 1 hour more than Patrick to complete the same journey. Find Saul's average speed for the whole journey.
    a. 54 miles per hour
    b. 55.7 miles per hour
    c. 60.2 miles per hour
    d. 78 miles per hour

52. It takes 5 workers 2 days to lay carpet in a house. If two of the workers are on vacation, how long will it take the remaining workers to lay the carpet?
    a. 2 ¾ days
    b. 3 days
    c. 3 ⅓ days
    d. 4 ¼ days

53. Five students are standing in a straight line. Bob is after Sue, but before Dee. Tom is not beside Sue and is after Bob. Joe is before Sue. Dee is after Tom. In which order are the students standing?
    a. Sue, Tom, Dee, Joe, Bob
    b. Joe, Sue, Bob, Tom, Dee
    c. Joe, Tom, Sue, Bob, Dee
    d. Dee, Tom, Sue, Bob, Joe

54. A toy store sells games board games for $11.98 each and sets of building blocks for $18.48 each. Select the best estimate for 3 board games and 2 sets of building blocks.
    a. $30.00
    b. $72.00
    c. $73.00
    d. $78.00

55. A taxi company charges $2.50 for the first mile and $0.50 for every subsequent mile or part thereof. Jacob travelled 9 ½ miles in a taxi. How much taxi fare did he owe?
    a. $4.50
    b. $5.50
    c. $7.00
    d. $8.00

56. Mrs. Moore invested $3,000 in Account A, which pays 6% interest annually, and $2,500 in Account B, which pays 8% interest annually. Which account earned more interest, and how much more did it earn?
    a. Account A at $20 more
    b. Account A at $180 more
    c. Account B at $20 more
    d. Account B at $200 more

57. Approximately what percentage of managers earns more than $26,584 annually?
    a. 10%
    b. 25%
    c. 75%
    d. 90%

58. Which of the following statements best describes the graph?
    a. Ten managers make $18,230 or less annually.
    b. Ninety percent of managers make $53,245 or above annually.
    c. A majority of managers earn between $26,584 and $46,161 annually.
    d. No managers earn more than $53,245 annually.

Use the following standardized test score report for a particular student to answer question 59.

Subject	Percentile Score
Reading Vocabulary	90
Reading Comprehension	85
Language Mechanics	88
Language Expression	83
Math Computation	92
Math Concepts and Application	89
Study Skills	78

59. Which of the following best explains the student's score on Language Mechanics?
    a. The student correctly answered eighty-eight percent of the Language Mechanics questions correctly.
    b. The student performed better than eighty-eight percent of other students his age on the Language Mechanics section of the test.
    c. The student missed twelve questions on the Language Mechanics section of the test.
    d. The student is a B student in Language.

60. If you randomly select one coin from a jar containing twelve pennies, thirteen nickels, eleven dimes, and sixteen quarters, what is the probability of selecting a penny?
    a. 1/3
    b. 2/5
    c. 3/13
    d. 39/52

61. A spinner has 12 equal sections numbered one through twelve. What is the probability of landing on an odd number?
    a. 1 out of 2
    b. 2 out of 3
    c. 2 out of 5
    d. 4 out of 12

History/Social Studies

62. A Native American people that the early European explorers would NOT have encountered on their visits to the West Indies were the:
    a. Totonacs.
    b. Ciboney.
    c. Caribs.
    d. Tainos.

63. The economy of colonial New England focused on manufacture and trade mainly because:
    a. soil and climate conditions in New England were not conducive to year-round farming.
    b. the New England colonists were primarily merchants from England and Scotland.
    c. slavery did not exist in the northern colonies.
    d. the New England colonists wanted to achieve economic dominance over the Middle Atlantic colonies.

64. The Sugar Act (1764), the Stamp Act (1765), and the Townshend Acts (1767-1770) all aroused the American colonists' concerns about:
    a. separation of powers.
    b. taxation without representation.
    c. the right to an impartial and speedy trial.
    d. freedom of speech.

65. The annexation of Texas by the United States in 1845 was:
    a. an effort to help stem the spread of slavery west of the Mississippi.
    b. part of an effort to fulfill Manifest Destiny.
    c. an expression of principles set forth in the Monroe Doctrine.
    d. an effort to improve relations between the United States and Mexico.

66. The end of Reconstruction was marked by which event?
    a. the assassination of Abraham Lincoln
    b. ratification of the 14th Amendment
    c. the impeachment of Andrew Johnson
    d. the withdrawal of federal troops from the South

67. A group that grew in numbers as a result of the Industrial Revolution was:
    a. small farmers.
    b. unskilled workers.
    c. skilled craftsmen.
    d. the rural population.

68. A major cause of the Great Depression of the 1930s was:
    a. the overproduction and underconsumption of consumer goods.
    b. the failure of industry to produce sufficient consumer goods.
    c. underproduction and rising prices in the agricultural sector.
    d. the reduction of import tariffs.

69. Who famously crossed the Rubicon in 49 BC?
    a. Julius Caesar
    b. Cleopatra
    c. Mark Antony
    d. Marcus Brutus

70. Which of the following peoples did not practice a form of feudalism?
    a. The Norsemen (Vikings)
    b. The Germans
    c. The Persians
    d. The Byzantines

71. Who was the first President of South Africa to be elected in a fully representative South African election?
    a. Mahatma Gandhi
    b. Thabo Mbeki
    c. Kgalema Motlanthe
    d. None of the above

72. Why did each Incan ruler have to earn his own fortune?
    a. A tradition that all the wealth an Incan king accumulated during his reign would be used to house and care for the king's mummified remains.
    b. A tradition that all of a deceased king's wealth would be added to the main Incan temple's treasury.
    c. A tradition that all of a deceased king's wealth would be used to create a large public work in the king's memory.
    d. A belief that the new king needed to prove his worth through conquest and adding to the royal treasury.

73. The first ships to set sail from Europe in the Age of Exploration departed from:
    a. Spain.
    b. the Netherlands.
    c. England.
    d. Portugal.

74. Which of the following is not a true statement concerning the beginnings of slavery in the Virginia colony?
    a. Slavery was established quickly as a means of securing a cheap source of labor.
    b. Initially slaves could become free through converting to Christianity.
    c. The number of slaves in Virginia increased as tobacco planters required a steady supply of labor.
    d. Early Virginian slaves included both Africans and Native Americans.

75. The strategy of containment was a major element of American foreign policy during:
    a. the Spanish-American War.
    b. World War I.
    c. World War II.
    d. the Cold War.

76. Which of the following is NOT useful in controlling soil erosion?
    a. crop rotation
    b. cattle grazing
    c. mulching
    d. reforestation

77. Article I of the United States Constitution includes the following paragraph:

    No title of nobility shall be granted by the United States: and no person holding any office of profit or trust under them, shall, without the consent of the Congress, accept of any present, emolument, office, or title, of any kind whatever, from any king, prince, or foreign state.

This paragraph most directly reflects the influence of:
    a. John Locke.
    b. Baron de Montesquieu.
    c. Jean-Jacques Rousseau.
    d. Thomas Paine.

78. Which of the following is most true regarding the Electoral College?
    a. The Electoral College requires that every voter's choice is directly represented in an election, thereby ensuring that the candidate with the largest popular vote wins the election.
    b. The Electoral College greatly affects Presidential campaigning, since candidates often target their campaign stops and advertising to specific states depending on the number and scope of their Electoral votes.
    c. The Electoral College consists of individuals appointed by the courts who are legally bound to vote for the candidates they represent.
    d. The Electoral College educates young voters about the responsibilities of citizenship and participation in general elections.

79. Which of these presidents most greatly expanded the power of the presidency?
    a. Thomas Jefferson
    b. Herbert Hoover
    c. Lyndon Johnson
    d. George W. Bush

80. The Tropic of Capricorn:
    a. separates the northern and southern hemispheres.
    b. separates the eastern and western hemispheres.
    c. is the southernmost latitude at which the sun can appear directly overhead at noon.
    d. is the northernmost latitude at which the sun can appear directly overhead at noon.

81. Which of these countries does NOT share a border with Israel?
    a. Jordan
    b. Saudi Arabia
    c. Lebanon
    d. Egypt

82. Most of the earliest civilizations flourished in or near what sort of geographic feature?
    a. Mountains
    b. Valleys
    c. Oceans
    d. Rivers

83. The two new states admitted under the Missouri Compromise of 1820 were Missouri and:
    a. Ohio
    b. Alabama
    c. Kansas.
    d. Maine

84. Most of the region known in ancient times as Mesopotamia is located in the present-day nation of:
    a. Iran.
    b. Saudi Arabia.
    c. Turkmenistan.
    d. Iraq.

85. The idea that the purpose of the American colonies was to provide Great Britain with raw materials and a market for its goods is an expression of:
    a. free trade.
    b. most favored nation status.
    c. mercantilism.
    d. laissez-faire capitalism.

86. The economist who focused on the potential for populations to grow faster than available food supplies was:
    a. Adam Smith.
    b. John Stuart Mill.
    c. Thomas Malthus.
    d. Friedrich Engels.

87. An economist who advocated government intervention to prevent and remedy recessions and depressions was:
    a. Adam Smith.
    b. John Maynard Keynes.
    c. Friedrich Hayek.
    d. Milton Friedman.

88. The power of Congress to regulate interstate commerce was the main issue argued in:
    a. Marbury v. Madison.
    b. Dartmouth College v. Woodward.
    c. McCulloch v. Maryland.
    d. Gibbons v. Ogden.

89. Which skill should all students possess upon matriculating from elementary school into middle school?
    a. The ability to identify different points of view related to a topic or event.
    b. The ability to distinguish the difference between a primary and secondary source.
    c. The ability to identify major eras in U.S. history, beginning with colonization.
    d. The ability to identify bias in written material.

90. Which of the following would not be considered a primary reason for population migration?
    a. Political or military conflict
    b. Natural disaster
    c. Unusually high birth rate
    d. High numbers of skilled workers

91. The main purpose of the census is to:
    a. monitor illegal immigration.
    b. apportion seats in the House of Representatives.
    c. help determine federal income tax rates.
    d. reapportion seats in the United States Senate.

Science

92. The main byproduct of photosynthesis is...
    a. Carbon dioxide
    b. Carbon monoxide
    c. Helium
    d. Oxygen

93. All living things have
    a. Organelles
    b. Cells
    c. Tissues
    d. Cell walls

94. In photosynthesis, what kind of chemical reaction transforms CO_2 into carbohydrates?
    a. Oxidation
    b. Chemiosmosis
    c. Reduction
    d. Hydrolysis

95. If animal dissection is unavailable or unacceptable within a particular environment, what might be an appropriate alternative to provide students with similar instruction?

  a. Large, colorful wall posters of relevant animals with detailed descriptions and anatomical labels.

  b. Selected readings about the history and ethics of animal dissection.

  c. Student participation in a CD-ROM, which contains a virtual dissection program.

  d. Student-drawn diagrams of animals, complete with realistic colors, proportions, and labels.

96. A purple-flowered pea plant is crossed with a white-flowered pea plant and all of the progeny are purple. The purple allele is _____ to white.

  a. Recessive

  b. Dominant

  c. Codominant

  d. Not enough information is given to tell.

97. An ecosystem consists of

  a. The abiotic environment

  b. A collection of populations

  c. A community of organisms and the physical environment

  d. Many populations of a species interacting with one another

98. What else could be added to these guidelines to help the students deepen their understanding of biodiversity?

  a. Always bring binoculars, since some organisms can be difficult to see with the human eye.

  b. Whenever possible, sketch or describe the connections and relationships between the living organisms in the environment.

  c. Be very quiet, so as not to startle any living organisms you may be observing.

  d. If necessary, take pictures or videos of interesting observations for later reference.

99. Which of the following is the most likely explanation for the reason finches on separate islands within an archipelago have differently shaped beaks?

  a. Each bird evolved from a pre-existing ancestor on each island.

  b. The finches spread among the islands, but in small numbers, so genetic drift caused beak shape to change.

  c. Natural selection shaped the beaks in accordance with food availability on each island.

  d. The different finches were introduced by ancient humans.

100. Which of the following is an example of speciation?

  a. A species of bird gradually develops a new color pattern due to environmental pressures

  b. A species of fish becomes extinct due to overfishing

  c. A species is rescued from extinction due to human intervention

  d. A new species forms after members of a single species become geographically isolated from one another

101. Which of the following are NOT known to cause genetic mutations?

  a. Antioxidants

  b. Errors in coding during DNA replication

  c. Viruses

  d. Radiation

102. The Big Bang Theory of the origin of the universe is supported by which of the following scientific observations?
    a. The existence of sonic booms
    b. The observation that other galaxies are moving away from our galaxy
    c. The existence of the aurora borealis
    d. The discovery of ancient fossils

103. What is the main type of chemical reaction in the sun?
    a. Nuclear fusion
    b. Nuclear fission
    c. Nucleation
    d. Hydrogenation

104. Which type of rock is formed by high temperatures and great pressures?
    a. Sedimentary rock
    b. Igneous rock
    c. Composite rock
    d. Metamorphic rock

105. Which of the following is NOT part of the carbon cycle?
    a. Respiration
    b. Sedimentation
    c. Transpiration
    d. Decomposition

106. Given the half-life of the following radioactive isotopes, which would be most useful for dating fossils?
    a. P32 – 14.2 days
    b. H3 – 4500 days
    c. C14 – 5740 years
    d. U235 – 700 million years

107. Which of the following properties of a meteorite moving through the planet's atmosphere would change as it approached the surface of the earth?
    a. Its mass
    b. Its volume
    c. Its density
    d. Its weight

108. Which of the following lessons would be the best set of examples illustrating the difference between scientific fact and theory?
    a. Big Bang and Laws of Motion
    b. Chaos theory and Evolution
    c. Conservation of Mass/Elasticity and Carbon-14 Dating
    d. Astronomical Wormholes and Black Holes

109. Which of the following is an example of chemical weathering in rocks?
    a. Erosion caused by contact with wind and water
    b. Cracking caused by interaction with ice or salt crystals
    c. Color change due to oxidation
    d. Both A and B

110. Plate tectonics affect humans in which of the following ways?
    a. It causes earthquakes and volcanoes, which necessitate specialized adaptations in building codes and safety regulations
    b. It makes some areas cooler and wetter than others, meaning that agriculture is more successful in some areas than others
    c. It causes desertification, which forces humans to migrate to areas with more hospitable climates.
    d. It has no discernable effect on humans

111. Which of the following does NOT contribute to the creation of ocean currents?
    a. Wind
    b. The moon's gravitational pull
    c. Ice cap and glacial melting
    d. The sun's heat

112. Of the following, which is the most basic unit of matter?
    a. A helium atom
    b. A sodium ion
    c. A proton
    d. An oxygen molecule

113. Which of the following changes in physical properties is a chemical change?
    a. Dissolving a seltzer tablet in water
    b. Grinding pepper into powder
    c. Freezing water
    d. Churning cream into butter

114. Which of the following substances is most likely to contain acetic acid?
    a. Cream of tartar
    b. Vinegar
    c. Baking powder
    d. Water

115. Use the information in the table above to identify the mathematical expression that could be used to correctly calculate the force of gravity in Newtons between Earth and its moon.

a. $F = \dfrac{(6.67 \times 10^{-11}) \times (7.36 \times 10^{22}) \times (5.9742 \times 10^{24})}{3.84 \times 10^{3}}$

b. $F = \dfrac{(9.81) \times (7.36 \times 10^{22}) \times (5.9742 \times 10^{24})}{3.84 \times 10^{3}}$

c. $F = \dfrac{(6.67 \times 10^{-11}) \times (3.84 \times 10^{3})}{(7.36 \times 10^{22}) \times (5.9742 \times 10^{24})}$

d. $F = \dfrac{(6.67 \times 10^{-11}) \times (7.36 \times 10^{22}) \times (5.9742 \times 10^{24})}{(9.81) \times (3.84 \times 10^{3})}$

116. The force of gravity on Earth's moon is 1/6 the force of gravity on the Earth. The force due to gravity on Earth is 9.81 m/s². What is the weight of a 5 kg mass on the moon?
    a. 0.833 N
    b. 8.175 N
    c. 30.00 N
    d. 49.05 N

117. Heating a liquid will most likely change its
    a. Crystal structure
    b. Density
    c. Mass
    d. Electrical conductivity

118. Which mathematical expression can be used to calculate the *total* resistance in a series circuit?
    a. $R_{eq} = R_1 + R_2 + \cdots + R_n$

    b. $\dfrac{1}{R_{eq}} = \dfrac{1}{R_1} + \dfrac{1}{R_2} + \cdots + \dfrac{1}{R_n}$

    c. $R = \dfrac{\rho l}{A}$

    d. $C = Q / V$

119. What unit describes the frequency of a wave?
    a. hertz (Hz)
    b. decibels (dB)
    c. meters (m)
    d. meters per second (m/s)

120. Which of the following is an example of nuclear fission?
    a. the formation of helium in our sun
    b. the atomic bombs used at the end of WWII
    c. the hydrogen bombs tested during the Cold War
    d. particles created in the Large Hadron Collider (LHC)

Answers and Explanations

Literature and Language Studies

1. B: According to extensive research on fluency rates, 200 words per minute is an above-average rate for a 7th grader. Words correct per minute (WCPM) scores measure fluency, not comprehension. Also, rapid decoding skills associated with high reading fluency scores are often associated with greater comprehension, but this is not always the case.

2. A: There are many reading inventories available to assess reading fluency in the classroom, but a teacher can get a general sense of whether a student has reading fluency problems by simply asking the student to read an unfamiliar grade-level text aloud and noting whether the student reads with appropriate speed, accuracy, and intonation for his or her grade level. If the student reads very fluently, then the problem clearly lies elsewhere, but if the student shows signs of poor fluency, then more in-depth testing is necessary.

3. A: Pausing periodically during reading to assess one's comprehension of the text is an example of metacognition, which is often defined as "thinking about thinking." Pausing to self-assess comprehension during reading is an important skill that is frequently referred to as "self-monitoring."

4. A: Providing books that resonate with students' interests and personal experiences will help increase their intrinsic motivation to read. Intrinsic motivation is a desire that arises from internal factors; it is the enjoyment of an activity for its own sake. Extrinsic motivation arises from factors such as a desire to gain material rewards. Intrinsic motivation is much more likely than external motivation to sustain a lifelong commitment to reading.

5. C: The most appropriate way for Ms. Sanchez to respond to this request would be to provide the parents with a list of books that are at the student's reading level. Because Ms. Sanchez knows the student's current reading level and interests, she can offer the most effective suggestions. It will be more difficult for the student's parents to find appropriate books on the Internet because they do not possess Ms. Sanchez' professional knowledge, and it would be impractical for them to ask other parents what their children are reading because their son is reading at a higher level than most of his peers.

6. D: It is true that, while film producers can influence the viewer's mood using music and lighting, writers must rely entirely on literary conventions to invoke emotion. However, both films and movies can be effective at persuading people to change their opinions, and both mediums can effectively address serious journalistic subject matter. .

7. B: While test scores can tell a teacher that a student is struggling, they cannot diagnose *why* the student is struggling. The fact that Brian says he hates reading suggests that his confidence and motivation have been negatively affected. The teacher will have to assess Brian's reading skills, including fluency and comprehension, in order to determine where he needs extra help. The best way to get an older student to comply with this kind of assessment is to ask him to read something he likes. Brian's selection of text will give the teacher clues about his current reading level, as will his verbal reading of it. The comprehension questions will help the teacher know whether or not the problem is just comprehension, or an additional skill that is affecting his comprehension.

8. A: Critical, or inferential, comprehension refers to a student's ability to understand what is not explicitly stated in a text. This kind of comprehension can be more challenging for students because the ideas are implied and not written or explained within a text. In choices B, C and D, students can identify or answer questions, the answer to which can be agreed upon based on that what is written. In choice A, however, readers will have to make an inference or interpretation in order to use the skill. In order to distinguish cause and effect, the read must utilize that which is written in the text and interpret the material.

9. C: When a class contains students of varying abilities, using group work is a helpful model. Within a group, each student can contribute and learn in a relatively low-pressure environment. Often, when asked to speak in front of the entire class, some students will lack confidence. To avoid one student's dominance of the group, or conversely, another student failing to contribute, the teacher has assigned each student a specific discussion topic. In this way, each student gets a chance to lead and a chance to learn. Choice A relies on worksheets to provide instruction; choice B relies on the stronger students to teach instead of helping them to grow as well. Choice D is a less-thorough version of choice C.

10. B: Students are presented with countless visual symbols and images every day through media and in shared cultural exchanges. In teaching the students about viewing and representing, teachers can help them deconstruct these symbols and understand their meaning, as well as monitor what messages the students themselves are sending. Choice A would likely help students represent the novel in class, but might not be as informative if the students cannot speak. It may also be boring for other students to watch a wordless play made from an entire novel. Choice C would be a great activity for students to learn about representing information; however, this choice does not address the question prompt saying that Mr. Hawking will be utilizing the current class reading.

11. A: A student response form measures two things: one, how fast a student will be able to read the story to himself and how well he will probably understand the text. In this kind of assessment, the teacher will be able to understand how a group of students might individually comprehend or move through a text ahead of time. This evaluation will allow the teacher to plan more effective lessons. Choice B refers to a kind of assessment in which a student will fill in blanks in a paragraph with words that make meaning out of what they have read. Choice C is not a commonly-used evaluation and choice D is a group-administered inventory.

12. D: Most students in grades 4 through 8 have mastered basic oral language skills, but teachers should still incorporate class activities designed to enhance higher-order oral language skills such as persuasion, summarizing, listening and responding appropriately to others' opinions, and engaging an audience.

13. A: A student who grasps the alphabetic principle understands that there is a systematic relationship between sounds and letters. Students begin to understand this concept when they learn the names and sounds of multiple letters, after which they learn to see those letters representing sounds within words.

14. C: A teacher who wants to get information about her students' specific strengths and weaknesses should administer an informal reading inventory such as the BRI, QRI-4, CRI-CFC, or ARI. Reading inventories not only provide the most up-to-date information about a student's reading skills, but they also allow the teacher to see the student read in real time and identify his or

her specific strengths and deficiencies. Test scores and grades can determine the student's overall reading ability, but not his or her specific strengths and weaknesses.

15. A: Writing an email in all capital letters is widely considered to be the online equivalent of shouting, and shouting is considered rude in Internet communications just like it is considered rude in face-to-face interactions. Video commenting is typically a very informal forum, and use of nonstandard punctuation is acceptable. Discussion boards are generally forums for conversation and exchange of ideas, and polite disagreement is acceptable in these forums.

16. D: There are three main types of reading comprehension: literal, inferential, and evaluative. Literal comprehension involves being able to grasp information that is directly stated in the text. Inferential comprehension involves combining prior knowledge with the information in the text to understand concepts that are implied or indirectly stated. Evaluative reading comprehension questions ask for the reader's opinion.

17. C: A teacher asking students to perform a brief reading comprehension activity and then providing immediate feedback on the students' performance is an example of guided practice. Guided practice involves practicing a skill in a controlled environment under the observation of the instructor who provides immediate feedback on how the skill was performed and how performance can be improved.

18. D: A student reading a text at his or her independent reading level should find it easy to read without outside assistance of any kind. Students should easily recognize 100 percent of the words in the text. Texts at the instructional reading level are more challenging and require outside assistance in order for students to fully comprehend them, but they are also below the frustration level, the point at which the student recognizes less than 95 percent of the words in the text.

19. D: Graphic organizers can be used for many purposes, such as helping students self-monitor as they read, assessing reading comprehension, and visually representing the text structure. They can also take many forms, including storyboards or Venn diagrams.

20. B: Providing explicit instruction in expository text comprehension as well as narrative text comprehension represents the most effective overall approach to helping students succeed in reading tasks required for math, science, and social studies. While it is helpful to offer students nonfiction texts and teach them about visual data representations, these are specific strategies and instructional objectives, not overall approaches.

21. C: Student journals can serve a variety of purposes if students are provided with the teacher's expectations. Journals are good examples of a student's writing progress throughout a given period of time. They also provide opportunities for students to express themselves through writing and drawing of many kinds. Students can also use journal assignments to practice specific writing skills. However, students should probably not be permitted to write freely without parameters, as this strategy would not always yield progress. Conversely, students will not feel motivated to write in journals if they are concerned about their grades.

22. C: There are six generally accepted traits of writing: ideas, word choice, sentence fluency, conventions, organization and voice. Writing conventions refer to aspects of writing that make the text easy to read. These conventions include spelling, punctuation, grammar, spacing and titles. Each choice in this question refers to some aspect of writing conventions except choice C. This

choice refers to an aspect of the "ideas" trait, and working on supporting details and their relationship to main concepts would not fall under the writing conventions category.

23. B: Student development is holistic and covers a spectrum of skills that are all developing simultaneously, and at different rates. Literacy development is not a linear process, nor can it be completely illustrated by one specific test. While standardized tests are convenient for providing a snapshot of development, they may not be the best tool for describing such a complex process. However, providing examples such as writing samples or reading fluency assessments will give a parent an idea of what the student is doing in class. The teacher can then provide information about how the student is progressing compared to other students of the same age. Choices C and D focus more on giving students and parents responsibility for improving skills instead of communicating progress thus far.

24. C: Pragmatics is a critical aspect of oral language development that involves understanding the social rules and overtones of conversation, as well as interpreting the nonverbal signals given by others. By participating in a small-group discussion and summarizing their discussion partners' comments, students will practice listening and interpreting others' oral comments.

25. B: The writing process typically contains six components, which include choices A, B, and D. Choice C is a style of writing that is related to the questions in the box. However, persuasive writing is not technically a part of the writing process; the writing process applies to all styles. In developing ideas, the student will decide what he wants to communicate about a given topic and how it should be communicated. This process precedes the organizational phase in that the student is focusing in on what is most important and eliminating information that is irrelevant to the topic.

26. A: This choice provides the most direct route for assessing a student's reading fluency and comprehension. Having the student read aloud is the best way to monitor all aspects of fluency, including speed, accuracy, and vocal expression. In asking questions at the end, the teacher will not be relegated to correct or incorrect answers written upon a page. He or she will be able to hear the student's vocalization, which may reveal degrees of understanding not found in a worksheet.

27. B: The SQ3R method is very helpful when applied to a text that a student needs to read for informational purposes. By previewing and formulating questions, the student learns to turn his or her attention to salient ideas and details in the text. Reading with the goal of answering questions and confirming initial impressions about what is important in the text adds another layer to this process. By making notes and reviewing, the student can solidify important information in order to take a test or retain said information in memory for class discussions. The multi-layered study approach is best applied to a larger reading assignment in which the student will need to process the information multiple times, which is not usually necessary with poetry, journals, or stories.

28. D: Graphic organizers, story trees, and story maps are just a few tools students can use to "study" as they read. Rather than detail the events and characters for the students, Mrs. Nelson should have the students help her make a story map that includes the major events in each part of the story to help them remember. Characterizations can also be detailed, perhaps with a drawing or a picture of the person to aid in retention. By doing this, Mrs. Nelson is teaching the students to create organization for themselves in a way that can be used again and again as they learn.

29. C: In this choice, the students are directly engaging in media deconstruction, which refers to the process of analyzing media images and determining their intended meanings. This project directly relates to the *viewing and representing* portion of the curriculum and will directly affect students'

- 75 -

ability to deconstruct modern-day images as well as academic and literary images. They will learn the difference between intended meaning and actual meaning and build their interpretive skills. Choice A may provide too much challenge and abstraction for 8th-graders. Choices B and D do not provide enough instruction to guide or build the students' skills and instead ask them to interpret and analyze without the benefit of guidance from the teacher. Choice C incorporates scaffolding and individual participation.

30. C: The Texas Essential Knowledge and Skills (TEKS) document for grades 4 through 8 states that students are expected to read grade-level texts fluently; however, the TEKS does not identify specific WCPM scores for each grade level. Instead, teachers are expected to use their professional knowledge and judgment to determine whether or not a student meets this standard.

Mathematics

31. C: 3/4 and 0.75
Explanation: $3 \div 4 = 0.75$
Three divided by four equals seventy-five hundredths.

32. A: 25%
Explanation: 25% = 1/4; Thea saved $10 off a $40 item. $10 is ¼, or 25%, of $40.
25% equals 25/100 which simplifies to 1/4. Subtract $30 from $40 to find that Thea saved $10 on the dictionary. $10/$40 simplifies to 1/4 which is the same as 25%.

33. C: 33
Explanation: $8 \times 4 + 6 \div 3 - 1 = (8 \times 4) + (6 \div 3) - 1 = 32 + 2 - 1 = 34 - 1 = 33$
By order of operations, first multiply and divide from left to right. 8 times 4 is 32, and 6 divided by 3 is 2. Then add and subtract from left to right. 32 plus 2 is 34, and 34 minus 1 is 33.

34. B: 296
Explanation: $(11 \times 29) + (15 \times 25) = 319 + 375 = 694$ total students; $694 - 398 = 296$ boys
First find the total number of children in the school: multiply 11 by 29 to get 319, and multiply 15 (26-11 = 15) by 25 to get 375. Add the two products (319 and 375) to find that there are 694 total students in the school. Subtract the number of girls (398) from 694 to determine that there are 296 boys in the school.

35. D: 2,460,234.75
Explanation: $4^2 + (15)^3 \times 9^3 - 5^4 \div 2^2 = 16 + 3375 \times 729 - 625 \div 4 = 16 + 2,460,375 - 625 \div 4 = 16 + 2,460,375 - 156.25 = 2,460,391 - 156.25 = 2,460,234.75$
First simplify the exponential numbers. $4^2=16$; $(15)^3=3375$; $9^3=729$; $5^4=625$; $2^2=4$; Multiply and divide left to right. 3,375 times 729 equals 2,460,375. 625 divided by 4 equals 156.25. Add and subtract left to right. 16 plus 2,460,375 equals 2,460,391. Subtract 156.25 from this sum to equal 2,460,234.75.

36. B: 32, 8
Explanation: The pattern consists of (4×12), $(4 \times 12) / 4$, (4×11), $(4 \times 11)/4$, (4×10), $(4 \times 10)/4$, (4×9), $(4 \times 9)/4$, $\underline{(4 \times 8) = 32}$, $\underline{(4 \times 8)/4 = 8}$.

37. C: y = 2x
Explanation: Substitute the x-coordinate point -1 into the equation; $2(-1) = -2$. Substitute the x-coordinate point 0 into the equation; $2(0) = 0$. Substitute the x-coordinate point 1 into the equation; $2(1) = 2$. Substitute the x-coordinate point 2 into the equation; $2(2) = 4$.

- 76 -

38. A: y = -x + 3
Explanation: Substitute the x-coordinate of point A (4) into the equation. –(4) + 3 = -1, so y = -1.
Substitute the x-coordinate of point B (3) into the equation. –(3) + 3 = 0, so y = 0.

39. B: Line B
Explanation: If y = 2x/x and x=1, then y = 2. If y = 2x/x and x = 2, then y = 2. If y = 2x/x and x=3,
then y =2.

40. C: 7/6
Explanation: Slope is the ratio of the difference between the y-coordinates and the x-coordinates of
a line. 10-3/ 7-1 = 7/6

41. D: 2
Explanation: 1^2 - 1/1 - 1 = 0/0; limit is 2.

42. D: 128
Explanation: Multiply 4 times 4 to find the area of one square face (4 in x 4 in = 16 in^2). Multiply 16
in^2 by 2 to find the total surface area for the square faces (16 in^2 x 2 = 32 in^2). Multiply 6 times 4 to
find the area of one rectangular face (6 in x 4 in = 24 in^2). Multiply 24 in^2 by 4 to find the total
surface area for the rectangular faces (24 in^2 x 4 = 96 in^2). Add the surface area of the square faces
to the surface area of the rectangular faces to find the total surface area of the box (32 in^2 + 96 in^2 =
128 in^2).

43. B: 93 x 10^6
Explanation: (10 x 10 x 10 x 10 x 10 x 10) x 93 = 1,000,000 x 93 = 93,000,000
10^6 equals 1 million; 10^6 x 93 = 93 million

44. A: 22,976 in^3
Explanation: 48 in x 30 in x 16 in = 23,040 in^3; 2in x 2in x 2in = 8in^3; 8in^3 x 8 = 64in^3; 23,040 in^3 -
64 in^3 = 22,976 in^3
Multiply 48 by 30 by 16 to find the volume of the block (23,040 in^3). Multiply 2 by 2 by 2 to find the
volume of the block taken from each corner (8 in^3). Multiply 8 in^3 by 8 (8 corners on a cube) to find
the total amount of volume removed (64 in^3). Subtract 64 in^3 from 23,040 in^3 to find the volume
that is left (22,976 in^3).

45. A: A direct proof starts with a set of certainties and states a series of logical facts to prove a
separate statement. Once x + y is expressed in a valid format that clearly has a factor of two (as
does 2(a+b+1)) it is certain that the sum of these two integers is even. Choice B contains a direct
assumption, and is therefore incorrect. Choice C begins to make valid point but skips to the
conclusion without clear explanation. Choice D makes no proof at all and simply restates the
original information.

46. A: The distributive property states that a(b+c)= ab + ac. Though the first half of the expression
contains a constant and a variable, the distributive property still applies. It is possible that the
associative or the commutative law can be applied when dealing with equations like this one, but
the transformation is made possible by the law of distribution.

- 77 -

47. B: $6.50y
Explanation: $3(\$y/2) = \$3y/2$; $\$2y \times 2 = \$4y$; $\$3y/2 + \$4y = \$11y/2 = \$5.50y$; $\$12y - \$5.50y = \$6.50y$
Multiply 3 times $y/2 to find the total amount spent on coffee ($3y/2). Multiply 2 by $2y to find the total amount spent on bagels ($4y). Add the coffee total to the bagel total to find the total amount of money Zac spent ($11y/2). Simplify this is $5.50y. Subtract $5.50y from $12y to find that Zac had $6.50y left.

48. C: add +5
Explanation: (-20 + +5 = -15), (-15 + +5 = -10), (-10 + +5 = -5). The sum of a negative number and a positive number gets closer to zero.

49. B: 8 minutes
Explanation: Multiply the time it takes Natalie to walk to school by the rate at which she walks (7 min x 80 feet/ minute = 560 feet/ minute). Divide the product by the new rate (560 feet/ minute ÷ 70 feet/ minute = 8 minutes) to find the new time.

50. C:

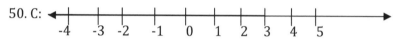

Explanation: $4x \le 12$. Divide both sides by 4 to get $x \le 3$. The line should begin at 3 and include all numbers less than 3.

51. B: 55.7 miles per hour
Explanation: Multiply 65 miles per hours by 6 hours to determine the total distance of the trip (65 x 6 = 390 miles). Divide 390 miles by Saul's time for the trip to find Saul's average speed (390 ÷ 7 = 55.7 miles per hour).

52. C: 3 ⅓ days
Explanation: The product of 5 men working two days equals the product of 3 men working y number of days. 5 x 2 = 3y; 10 = 3y. Divide both sides of the equation by 3 to determine how many days it takes 3 men to lay the carpet. 10/3 = 3y/3; 3 ⅓ = y.

53. B: Joe, Sue, Bob, Tom, Dee
Explanation: Bob must be between Sue and Dee, and Tom is after Bob. Joe must be at the front of the line, and Dee must be at the back of the line, because she is after Tom.

54. B: $72.00
Explanation: Round $11.98 to $12.00 and multiply by 3 ($12 x 3 = $36). Round $18.48 to $18 and multiply by 2 ($18 x 2 = $36). Find the sum of $36 and $36 ($36 + $36 = $72).

55. C: $7.00
Explanation: Multiply $0.50 by 9 as the problem stated that parts of miles are charged as full miles ($0.50 x 9 = $4.50). Add $4.50 to $2.50 to find the total amount of the taxi fare ($4.50 + $2.50 = $7.00).

56. C: Account B at $20 more
Explanation: Multiply $3000 by 0.06 find the amount of interest earned by Account A ($3000 x 0.06 = $180). Multiply $2500 by 0.08 to find the amount of interest earned by Account B ($2500 x 0.08 = $200). Subtract the amount of interest earned by Account A from the amount earned by Account B to determine how much more interest Account B earned ($200 - $180 = $20.)

57. C: 75%
Explanation: Twenty-five percent of managers earn $26,584 annually, so approximately 75% of managers earn more than $26,584 annually.

58. C: A majority of managers earn between $26,584 and $46,161 annually.
Explanation: The curve tops out between $26,584 and $46,161, which means that the majority of managers earn an annual salary between these amounts.

59. B: The student performed better than eighty-eight percent of other students her age on the Language Mechanics section of the test.
Explanation: The student scored in the 88th percentile on the Language Mechanics section of the test which means that she performed better than eighty-eight percent of other students her age .

60. C:.3/13
Explanation: Find the sum of the total number of coins (12 + 13 + 11 + 16 = 52). 12 out of 52 coins are pennies. 12/52 = 3/13.

61. A: 1 out of 2
Explanation: Six out of 12 numbers are odd, so there is a 1 out of 2 chance of landing on an odd number.

History/Social Studies

62. A: While the Ciboney, Caribs, and Tainos were indigenous to the islands of the West Indies, the Totonacs lived in Mexico. They are sometimes credited with founding the ancient city of Teotihuacan.

63. A: Agriculture was not a viable economic model for New Englanders. Although the colonists were mainly from England and Scotland, few were merchants before arriving in the colonies. Slavery existed in the north, although it was less important to the economy than it was in the agricultural south. New England colonists were not actively competing with their neighbors to the immediate south.

64. B: All of these acts of Parliament were intended to raise revenue at the expense of the colonies. The colonists challenged Parliament's right to levy tax on them without their express consent.

65. B: The term "Manifest Destiny" originated with the annexation of Texas as Americans began to envision a nation that spread from coast to coast. Texas entered the union as a slave state. The Monroe Doctrine addressed European intervention in the Western Hemisphere, which was not an issue in the annexation of Texas. Mexican resentment of the annexation was a factor in the Mexican War, which began the following year.

66. D: The last federal troops were removed from the South in 1877 following the inauguration of Republican President Rutherford B. Hayes. The goals of reunifying the country and establishing functional state governments in the South were not marked by Lincoln's assassination in 1865, ratification of the 14th Amendment in 1868, or the 1868 impeachment of Andrew Johnson.

67. B: As production shifted to factories, large number of unskilled workers were needed to operate the machinery that was beginning to put many skilled craftsmen out of work. As farms grew larger

and increasingly mechanized, the number of people who owned their own farm began to decrease. The rural population declined as people flocked to the cities in search of employment.

68. A: Along with stock market speculation, a major cause of the Great Depression was an increased supply of cars, radios, and other goods that was not matched by consumer demand. Industrial production far exceeded the population's purchasing power. Farmers were plagued by overproduction and falling prices while international trade suffered from rising tariffs.

69. A: In 50 BC, Julius Caesar was called back to Rome by the Roman Senate in order to stand trial for treason and corruption. When he reached the Rubicon, he decided to ignore Roman Law and the Mos Maiorum (uncodified tradition with nearly the force of law), and instead took one legion to Rome with him, famously uttering the words "the die is cast." This was the beginning of a chain of events that led to the creation of the first Roman triumvirate and the transition of Rome from a Republic to an Empire, with Julius Caesar as "Perpetual Dictator," until his murder in the Senate. His adopted son Octavius (later taking the regnal name "Augustus") eventually became the first emperor.

70. A: Feudalism was a common practice during the Middle Ages, popular as a means of providing social structure and for maintaining the established government and social order. It was most widespread and systemic in Europe but also practiced in other parts of the world including Persia and the Byzantine Empire.

The Norsemen of what is now known as Scandinavia, however, were an exception to European feudalism and lived in a fairly egalitarian society where rank was strongly based on personal merit. This is not to say that the Norsemen were entirely opposed to the class delineations of feudalism; when the French King Charles the Simple ceded to them the land that became the province of Normandy, the Norsemen who settled there settled into a feudalistic structure that their descendants took with them to England during the Norman Conquest, where the feudal system was used to assist with subduing the newly-conquered English people.

71. D: Nelson Mandela was the first President of South Africa to be elected in a fully representative South African election. He was succeeded by Thabo Mbeki, who was succeeded by Kgalema Motlanthe. Mahatma Gandhi was an Indian who lived in South Africa for a time and greatly influenced Nelson Mandela. He was also the leader of India's independence movement.

72. A: The Incan civilization was very wealthy and the Incan rulers' individual wealth was used to care for their mummified remains following their deaths in order to emphasize the king's divinity as descendants of the Incan sun god Inti. When an Incan king died not only would his wealth be used to care for his remains, there would also be human sacrifices as the king's servants and favorite wives would be sacrificed so that they could continue serving him in the afterlife.

73. D: The Portuguese prince called Henry the Navigator launched the Age of Exploration with his voyage of 1419. He was followed by such notable Portuguese sailors as Bartholomeu Dias and Vasco de Gama, but Portuguese fortunes waned in the ensuing centuries as Spanish and Dutch exploration gained in prominence.

74. A: The historical evidence shows that the initial workers on tobacco plantations in Virginia were primarily indentured servants who would eventually receive their freedom. The path to slavery in its later forms was gradual, beginning with slavery as a form of punishment for legal infractions. Massachusetts became the first colony to legalize slavery in 1641, followed by other states,

including Virginia. This was followed by laws declaring that any children born to a slave mother would be slaves themselves in 1662 and a later decision that all persons who were not Christians in their "native country" would be slaves in 1705.

75. D: Formulated during the Truman administration and enduring throughout the Cold War, the policy of containment was intended to prevent the spread of Communism after World War II. It served as a rationale for many military decisions during the Korean and Vietnamese conflicts.

76. B: Overgrazing increases erosion by reducing the vegetation that naturally protects the soil from rain and wind. Rotating crops, applying mulch, and planting trees all serve to protect the soil and minimize erosion.

77. D: In his extremely influential pamphlet *Common Sense*, Paine argued persuasively against all forms of monarchy and aristocracy. He advocated the formation of a republic that derives its power exclusively from the governed. While the European writers also advocated government that derives its authority from the people, none went as far as Paine in proposing the total abolition of the traditional noble classes.

78. B: The Electoral College consists of individuals who represent the popular vote. Each state is allotted a number of electoral voters based upon its representation in Congress. Once the general public has voted, the electoral voters cast their votes directly for President. States are given the freedom to choose electors according to their own specifications, and sometimes legally require the electors to vote for the candidates they support. Often, Presidential candidates will spend more time campaigning in states with larger numbers of electoral votes, or in states they believe will be crucial to winning the election. This process sometimes comes at the expense of states with smaller numbers, which do not hold early primaries, or are not deemed pivotal in the election process.

79. C: Johnson exerted his presidential power to advance the Great Society agenda and to enact major civil rights legislation. He also conducted a war in Vietnam without Congressional declaration. Jefferson, Hoover, and Bush were all outspoken advocates of limiting the role of government, including the executive branch.

80. C: Lying at a little more than 23° south of the equator, the Tropic of Capricorn is the border between the Southern Temperate Zone to the south and the Tropical Zone to the north. The southern hemisphere is tilted toward the sun to its maximum extent each year at the winter solstice in December. The northernmost latitude at which the sun can appear directly overhead is at the Tropic of Cancer during the summer solstice. The northern and southern hemispheres are separated by the equator at 0° degrees latitude. The eastern and western hemispheres are separated by the prime meridian at 0° longitude.

81. B: Although both Israel and Saudi Arabia border on the Gulf of Aqaba, Jordan stands between Israel and its giant neighbor to the southeast.

82. D: Early civilizations flourished alongside rivers such as the Nile in Egypt, the Euphrates in Mesopotamia, and the Yellow River in China. Besides providing the ancient settlers with a water source, these rivers also provided the land with the rich and fertile silt that the rivers deposited during their regular flooding cycles, making large scale agriculture possible for the ancient peoples.

83. D: Under the Missouri Compromise, Maine would be admitted as a free state while Missouri would enter as a slave state. Slavery would be prohibited in the former Louisiana Territory north of the 36°30' parallel except in the new state of Missouri. Ohio had entered the Union in 1803 under the Northwest Ordinance. Alabama had been admitted as a slave state shortly before the Missouri Compromise. After years of bloody conflict, Kansas entered the Union as a free state in 1861.

84. D: Lying between the Tigris and Euphrates rivers, the Mesopotamian region gave rise to many prominent cultures. Today, the land belongs mainly to Iraq while extending to parts of northeastern Syria, southeastern Turkey, and southwestern Iran.

85. C: Mercantilism is the economic theory that nations advance the goal of accumulating capital by maintaining a balance of trade such that the value of exports exceeds that of imports. Great Britain maintained colonies to provide an inexpensive source of raw materials while creating markets for the goods manufactured in England. Under free trade, governments refrain from hindering the international exchange of goods and services. Nations that are granted most favored nation status are assured of enjoying equal advantages in international trade. A laissez-faire capitalist economy would theoretically be completely free of government regulation.

86. C: Formulated in the early 19th century, Malthus's theory that population increase would ultimately outpace increases in the means of subsistence did not anticipate technological advances in food production and birth control; nevertheless, the theory was highly influential in the formulation of subsequent economic and social policies.

87. B: Keynesian economics is based on the notion that governments can effectively stimulate economic growth through taxation, adjustment of interest rates, and the funding of public projects. His economic philosophy contrasts sharply with the free-market philosophies of Smith, Hayek, and Friedman.

88. D: In Gibbons v. Ogden, the Supreme Court concluded that the power to regulate interstate commerce was granted to Congress by the Commerce Clause of the Constitution. The decision went on to say that federal law took precedence over any contrary state laws in regard to interstate trade. Marbury v. Madison (1803) addressed the issue of judicial review. Dartmouth College v. Woodward (1819) concerned the power of the federal court to overturn state law. McCulloch v. Maryland (1819) bolstered the doctrine of implied powers.

89. A: By the 5th grade, students should have been exposed to the concept of point of view. They should understand that various individuals will possess different perspectives on the same topic or event; additionally, teachers should illustrate how the United States has evolved from the desire to embrace different points of view, generally speaking. Choice B refers to research and inquiry skills that are taught toward the beginning of the high school curriculum. Choice C is usually found in middle-school lessons. The final choice relies on the ability to understand different points of view, but is typically taught in middle-school, following the initial lessons mentioned in choice A.

90. C: Populations will move or migrate for a variety of reasons, which are usually circumstances that significantly lower quality of life. The first two choices are obvious examples of negative scenarios leading residents to move to better locations. Choice D can be misleading in that it seems like a positive circumstance. However, high numbers of skilled workers can diminish the number of available jobs for all residents. The increased level of competition may result in population changes as people move away, searching for better jobs. High birth rates may eventually lead to large numbers of skilled workers, but usually do not bear direct correlation to migration rates.

91. B: Article I of the Constitution mandates the taking of a census every ten years. The purpose was to be sure that each state was proportionately represented in Congress according to its population as specified in the Constitution. Census data is also used to allocate federal funding for various programs and for shaping economic policies. Individual data collected by the U.S. Bureau of the Census is kept confidential for seventy-two years and does not affect income tax rates. Every state has two seats in the Senate regardless of population.

Science

92. D: The main byproduct of photosynthesis is oxygen. During photosynthesis, plants take in carbon dioxide, convert it into organic compounds like sugars, and release oxygen back into the atmosphere.

93. B: Cells are the basic units of life, and all organisms have them. Some organisms like bacteria have just a single cell, while complex organisms like humans have hundreds of trillions. Prokaryotes do not have organelles a. Not all organisms have tissues, groups of cells that make up connective tissue, muscle tissue, etc. Finally, only some types of cells, including plant cells, have cell walls d.

94. C: Photosynthesis can be represented by the following equation: $6CO_2 + 6H_2O \rightarrow C_6H_{12}O_6 + 6O_2$. A reduction reaction transforms CO_2 into glucose ($C_6H_{12}O_6$), a type of carbohydrate. An oxidation reaction a. is what transforms the water into oxygen. Chemiosmosis b. describes the movement of ions across cell membranes, and hydrolysis d. is a type of reaction in which water is separated into hydrogen and hydroxide ions.

95. C: The purpose of animal dissection in classrooms where this practice is used is to teach students about life processes, anatomy and physiology. Dissection is the most real way to illustrate these concepts because students can observe first-hand as they work. The CD-ROM program is mostly closely aligned with these goals of realism, since students will experience the same phenomena virtually.

96. B: Since all of the offspring are purple, the purple allele must be dominant, and the purple plant must be homozygous. The Punnett square would look like this (R is purple, r is white):

	R	R
r	Rr	Rr
r	Rr	Rr

If purple was recessive a. to white (white was dominant), at least some of the plants would be white. If the alleles were codominant c., the flowers would be light purple or contain both colors. Since b. is correct, d. is incorrect.

97. C: An ecosystem is an environment that includes both the physical environment and the plants, animals, and other organisms that reside within it. By definition, an ecosystem consists of both the abiotic a. and biotic environment. An ecosystem does not need to contain a collection of population b.; it could consist of an environment with only one population. Ecosystems can (and often do) contain more than a single species d.

98. B: One of the key concepts of biodiversity is the interconnectedness of living things. If students are visiting a natural environment, they will observe plants, animals, air and water phenomenon, as

- 83 -

well as any non-natural environmental factors. In keeping a field journal, students will deepen their understanding of all these factors. Ideally, they will also start to note the relationships between living things and understand that none of them would survive without the others. Noting the relationships and effects organisms have upon one another will be an important part of keeping their journals.

99. C: Finches with beaks well-suited for the types of food available on an island had an evolutionary advantage. As a result, these finches survived and reproduced, a phenomenon known as natural selection. The finches share a common ancestor, regardless of the island on which they now live a.. Genetic drift refers to genetic changes that occur due to random chance; this would not account for different beaks on different islands b. Introduction by humans would not account for different beaks d., since phenotypes change over time.

100. D: The formation of a new species after the members of a single species become geographically isolated from one another is an example of speciation. Speciation is the evolution of a completely new species, and usually results from environmental changes that affect two segments of a single population differently.

101. A: Viruses, errors in DNA replication, and radiation can all cause genetic mutations, but antioxidants are not known to cause mutations. Genetic mutations are typically harmful or neutral in their effects, but some mutations can prove beneficial.

102. B: The Big Bang Theory of the origin of the universe is supported by the observation that other galaxies are moving away from our galaxy. This observation is consistent with one of the observable predictions of the theory: that the universe is expanding. The presence of cosmic background radiation is also considered to be evidence in support of the theory.

103. A: Most of the sun's energy is produced by a nuclear fusion reaction. During these reactions, hydrogen atoms react to produce helium and energy, which we perceive as visible light. Nuclear fission occurs when atoms are broken apart b. Nucleation c. is a process that occurs during the formation of crystals, and hydrogenation d. is the reaction that results when H_2 is added to a solution.

104. D: Metamorphic rock is found deep beneath the surface of the earth, and is an important component of the earth's crust. This type of rock is formed at temperatures of up to 200°C. The formation also requires great amounts of pressure, which is often exerted by layers above the metamorphic rock. Sedimentary rock a. is formed by particles that settle on land or in water. Igneous rock b. is cooled, solidified magma, and the term composite c. does not describe a type of rock.

105. C: The carbon cycle is defined as the movement of the earth's carbon through organisms, oceans, air, rocks, and soil. Animals breathe out carbon dioxide during respiration a., which deposits carbon into the air. Carbon from the atmosphere is dissolved in sea water, and can settle on the ocean floor. This collected matter is known as sedimentation b. When organisms die, the carbon in their bodies is returned to the soil through decomposition d. Transpiration, the process by which plants lose water, does not transport carbon.

106. D: A half life of a radioactive isotope is the length of time it takes for the amount of an isotope present to decline by half. Some animal fossils are hundreds of millions of years old. Therefore, a U235 isotope would be most useful since it has the greatest half life. If one gram was present

initially, half a gram would still be present after 700 million years. The half lives of a., b., and c. are too short to date very old fossils.

107. D: An object's weight is actually a measure of the gravitational force acting on that object. In this case, as the meteorite moves towards earth's surface, the gravitational force on it would be greater. In other words, it would weigh more. The mass of the meteorite a. refers to the amount of matter it contains, which remains the same regardless of its location. Volume b. (the amount of space the meteorite occupies) and density c. (mass per unit of volume) would also stay the same.

108. A: A scientific theory is a dynamic set of ideas that attempt to explain a scientific phenomenon. Scientific theories are not proven fact; scientific facts, or laws, are based in proof and concrete knowledge about our world and cannot be disproven. Choice A lists a theory, the Big Bang, which refers to a set of ideas about the origin of the universe. The laws of motion are proven facts that explain the behavior or objects in our environment. Choices B and D both list sets of theories without facts. Choice C shows two scientifically accepted facts, those of mass and electricity conservation and the process of carbon-14 dating of objects.

109. C: Color change due to oxidation is a clear example of the chemical weathering of rocks. Cracking due to interactions with ice and salt crystals, as well as erosion caused by contact with the elements, are examples of physical weathering.

110. A: Plate tectonics affects human settlement by creating zones where events such as earthquakes and volcanoes are more likely, resulting in specialized adaptations in building codes and safety regulations. It does not directly affect climate.

111. C: Currents are basically the horizontal movement of water in the earth's oceans. Numerous forces act on the oceans to produce currents. Wind a. blowing on the surface causes movement because it pushes the water. Water heated by the sun expands d., which causes movement, and the moon is responsible for the ocean's tides and the resulting tidal currents. Ice cap and glacial melting c. causes ocean levels to rise vertically, but does not influence the horizontal movement of ocean water.

112. C: The most basic units of matter are protons, electrons, and neutrons. Protons are found in the nucleus, and have a positive charge. They are one of the three components of a helium atom a. When atoms have positive or negative charges, they are known as ions b. Molecules of oxygen, water, etc. d. are even more complex, consisting of one or more atoms held together by bonds.

113. A: Dissolving a seltzer tablet in water is an example of a chemical change since a new substance is produced. In this case, carbon dioxide is produced as a result of the reaction. Grinding pepper b. and freezing water c. merely changes the form of these substances, not their composition. Churning butter d. is a physical change. The globules of milk fat are broken apart so they can clump together and form butter. Although butter looks different than cream, they are composed of the same substances.

114. B: Acetic acid is a weak organic acid with a chemical formula of CH_3COOH. It is characterized by its sour taste and strong smell. Vinegar is a diluted form of acetic acid. Cream of tartar a. is a type of acid salt used in cooking. Its chemical formula is $KC_4H_5O_6$, and it does not contain acetic acid. Baking powder c. is a mixture of a salt and an acid, but it does not contain acetic acid. Water d. is neutral and its formula is H_2O.

115. A: The test taker who chooses a correctly combined the information in the table and recognized that the Universal Law of Gravitation is an inverse square law that relates the mass of the two bodies, the square of the distance between them, and the gravitational constant (G):

$$F = \frac{G(m_1 \times m_2)}{r^2}$$

The test taker who chooses b used the force of Earth's gravity instead of the gravitational constant.
The test taker who chooses c inverted the masses and the distance in the formula.
The test taker who chooses d modified the gravitational constant by a factor related to Earth's gravity (i.e. divided by Earth's gravity).
The test taker who chooses e combined the errors described above for c and d.

116. B: Weight is the force of gravity acting on a mass. The combination of Newton's 1st and 2nd Laws of Motion yields the mathematical formula F = ma. Applied to weight, this relationship can also be expressed as F = mg. To arrive at the correct answer, first multiply Earth's gravity by 1/6 to calculate the gravity on the moon (g = 9.81 m/s^2 x 1/6 = 1.635 m/s^2). The second step is to multiply this value by the mass of the object (F = 5 kg x 1.635m/s^2; F=8.175N).
The test taker who chooses a multiplied the mass by 1/6 and ignored the gravity component altogether. The test taker who chooses c divided the mass by 1/6 and ignored the gravity component altogether. The test taker who chooses d calculated the mass of the object on Earth and ignored the variable of the moon. The test taker who chooses e multiplied Earth's gravity by 6 instead of dividing it by 6.

117. B: Heating a liquid is most likely to change its density, a measure of mass per unit of volume. Water, for instance, has a density of 1g/cm^3 at 4°C. As it is heated and molecules become more spread apart, the density decreases. In general, liquids do not have a crystal structure a. A liquid's mass, or the amount of matter it contains c. , will not change according to temperature, nor will its electrical conductivity d.

118. A: This expression can be used to calculate the total resistance in a series circuit. Choice b is the mathematical expression to calculate total resistance in a parallel series. Choice c is the mathematical expression to calculate resistance in a uniformly shaped material. Choice d is the mathematical expression to calculate capacitance (stored electric charge). Choice e is the mathematical expression to calculate capacitance in a parallel circuit.

119. A: Hertz (Hz) is a unit of measure of wave frequency.
The loudness of a sound is related to the amplitude of the wave and is measured in decibels (dB).
Wavelength is measured in meters (m).
Wave velocity is measured in meters per second (m/s).
Meters per second squared (m/s^2) is a measure of acceleration and has no real relevance to a discussion of waves.

120. B: The only example of nuclear fission. The nuclear reaction in the stars, including our sun (a), is a nuclear fusion reaction. Hydrogen bombs (c) are also examples of nuclear fusion. The Large Hadron Collider (d) and the Stanford Linear Accelerator Center (e) do not operate by means of nuclear reactions.